WORDS
THAT CHANGED
HISTORY

Dino J. Pedrone

and

Jonathan Pedrone

Cover design by Adam Pedrone.

WestBow Press books may be ordered through booksellers or by contacting:

WestBow Press
A Division of Thomas Nelson & Zondervan
1663 Liberty Drive
Bloomington, IN 47403
www.westbowpress.com
1 (866) 928-1240

ISBN: 978-1-9736-6292-1 (sc)
ISBN: 978-1-9736-6291-4 (e)

Print information available on the last page.

WestBow Press rev. date: 6/19/2019

DEDICATION

From Dino:

I am dedicating this book to my precious wife,
Roberta Dee (Bobbi) Pedrone.
You are an incredible wife, influential mother, and
Godly example to hundreds of people.
Thank you for allowing me to be your husband and
for the example of facing life with dignity, charm,
and hope for all of us. You are simply the best.

From Jonathan:

For Karen,
My Pearl, you have taught me more about the love and compassion of Jesus than any book ever could. The words in this book would not be possible without your love and support. I never want to learn to live my life without you.

CONTENTS

Words . . . 1
Beginning . . . 7
Legend . . . 13
Birthday . . . 21
Exile . . . 29
Coal . . . 41
Father . . . 45
Midrash . . . 49
Exchange . . . 61
Rock . . . 65
Spit . . . 77
Water . . . 87
Light . . . 93
Shoes . . . 97
Children . . . 105
4-Out-Up . . . 109
Image . . . 121
Tyrant . . . 135
Judas . . . 151
Left-Behind . . . 163
Tetelestai . . . 171
Messy . . . 177
Arrival . . . 183
GPS . . . 187
Napkin . . . 193

WORDS

"Jesus comes not for the super-spiritual, but for the wobbly and the weak-kneed who know they don't have it all together, and who are not too proud to accept the handout of amazing grace."[1]
--Brennan Manning

"Jesus did many other miraculous signs in the presence of his disciples which are not recorded in this book."
--John 20:30

"I SURVIVED HERMENEUTICS".

I can still remember the first time I (Jonathan) saw someone wearing a shirt on campus with those words on the front of their t-shirt. At first I assumed that maybe the shirt was a reference to an inside joke or possibly a t-shirt from a concert by a band named hermeneutics. Seeing the shirt on one student piqued my attention, but it was not until I saw two other students walking around campus together with the exact same shirt on that I became intrigued as to what sort of club they belonged to that granted them the privilege of wearing this shirt.

This occurred during my first semester of college, and eager to fit in and make new friends, I stopped the two students and inquired about where they purchased the shirts they were wearing. I tried to hide my extreme ignorance about what the word "hermeneutics" meant, and thankfully they were more than willing to explain to me where they got the shirts. They told me there was a class that students at the college could take, that was so difficult that the professor actually printed shirts at the end of the class that only students who passed the class were allowed to purchase and wear. These shirts were a badge of honor for

[1] Manning, Brennan. *The Ragamuffin Gospel: Embracing the Unconditional Love of God*. Portland, OR: Multnomah Books, 2005. 28.

a semester spent inside the library for long hours writing the myriad of papers that were required for the course. They told me that the course was so difficult and demanding that at the completion of the course almost every student bought a shirt to wear as a badge of honor.

The students must have seen the look of dread on my face. I was in my very first semester of college and was very unsure of where the library was even located, much less how to do research. I knew that I would avoid this class at all costs; I immediately considered taking the class over the shortened summer semester where the workload would be reduced.

On the first day of my second semester of college I can still remember sitting down for my Tuesday class. I was there 5 minutes early so I made small talk with a student sitting next to me. We asked each other about our course load, majors, and where we were in terms of our college careers. At approximately 9 AM, the professor strode to the front of the classroom and wrote three words that would change my semester:

"Welcome to hermeneutics."

I immediately panicked. I riffled through my backpack and found my registration for the semester; I thought that maybe I had wandered into the wrong class. I checked my schedule and looked at the course I had registered for. My registration was clear: BI 211: Biblical Interpretation (3 credits). Clearly I was not registered for a class on hermeneutics, and immediately considered how I could quietly escape the classroom without being noticed. Unfortunately I had chosen a seat in the middle of the classroom, and there was no way to sneak out of the classroom without everyone knowing that I was the person who had wandered into the wrong classroom on the first day, the walk of shame I deemed too embarrassing to follow through with.

After the professor wrote those words on the board, he turned and welcomed us to the course Biblical Interpretation. It was then that it dawned on me; hermeneutics was a fancy word for how to interpret the Bible. My ignorance caused me to sign up for a course that I had vowed to avoid at all costs and all because I didn't know the meaning of the word hermeneutics. The syllabus was daunting, every week we would have a project due, some of the projects sounded so strange that I was sure they were written in another language.

On the second day of class finding a seat was not an issue because about a third of the students in class on Tuesday had dropped the course. I seriously considered dropping the course in favor of the summer option, but something inside me wanted to see if I could complete the challenge. I decided that week to stick it out and earn my t-shirt. I can still remember clearly the final day of the class, our only responsibility was to show up outside of the professor's office door before 9:15AM and drop off our final project. My project (on the New Testament book of Jude) ended up about 35 pages in length. Combined with the other papers I had written for the class, I wrote nearly 75 pages that semester for a single class. Outside of the professor's office door was a small table with a bowl of candy and a stack of projects. I dropped my project on the table and enjoyed that piece of candy like no other piece of candy I have ever eaten. I was finished, I had survived hermeneutics, and I even got a shirt.

If you were to ask me today about the most memorable and the most informative course I took as a college student throughout undergraduate and into graduate studies, I would immediately reference this class. This was one of the most difficult courses I ever encountered but also one of the most beneficial.

It was in this class that I truly fell in love with understanding the story of the Bible, the nuances, the history, the story beneath the story that made the words come alive. In that class I was introduced to the dramatic, challenging, subversive text that we call Scripture. In the process I came to understand the beautiful, complex, challenging, disruptive, and nurturing words in the Bible.

I learned that Paul in 1 Thessalonians 1:1 refers to his fellow missionary as Silvanus, and not Silas, and how that small word change really matters to the original recipients of the book. I learned that despite what I had always been taught about the birth story of Jesus, that there was no actual hotel owner who turned Joseph and Mary away from the "inn" (Greek: Kataluma).[2] This word did not refer to a hotel, but rather a guest room that was most likely occupied by other members of Joseph's immediate family. And I learned that the book of Jude contains

---

[2] Farstad, Arthur L. *The NKJV Greek English Interlinear New Testament: Features Word Studies & New King James Parallel Text.* Nashville, TN: T. Nelson Publishers, 1994.

some very strange extra-biblical stories that are found in no other book in the Bible (Jude 6, 9, 14).

Since the day I first read in horror those three little words on the board "welcome to hermeneutics," I have been captivated by the Bible. Over twenty years later that interest has not dissipated. The challenges, joy, love, and disruption the Bible causes in my own life continues. And yes, I got the t-shirt.

I (Dino) walked across the campus of the Bible College I had enrolled in and met a group of college seniors who very politely welcomed me to the institution. The foliage in the air had the aroma of the fall that was typical of America's northeast reminding us that frost and cold were the on the way. This day, however, was sunny which gave students the opportunity to chat with classmates and new attendees on the sidewalks surrounding this old institution. The year was 1967. I joined the little huddle of upperclassmen desiring to fit in and, perhaps, even make a contribution to the discussion. I quickly found out these seniors were very gracious, but also rather authoritative with the knowledge they had learned over their previous years through scholarly professors.

Now, I had been brought up with good parents who took me to church, and I had a basic understanding of my belief system. However, this conversation had me bewildered. They were talking about something that was pre and another that was post something, and then there was a third option which they referred to as amillennialism. This was a fascinating conversation, but I was clueless. Then it happened. I knew nothing about this topic but I did want to impress these budding theologians. The unthinkable occurred. They asked me a question.

"Dino, are you a premillennialist, postmillenialist, or ammilenialist?"

My ignorance was now on display. I had no idea what they were talking about. I assumed what they believed they had learned at the college, therefore, I would probably believe the same thing. "What are you guys?" "We are all premillenialists." They said. I quickly responded: "Me too".

I left the group trying to give the impression that I needed to go and do something important. The fact is I did not want to be asked another question. I figured I could be on the team in this subject and figure it out later. Later that day I found a Bible professor at the college, and asked him if he could explain to me in simple terms what the discussion was about. Very politely and with a smile that could only be interpreted that his assignment was to give me a quick thorough answer on a subject that the best of Bible professors have debated for centuries. He spoke about five minutes. Frankly, I had very little idea of what he was talking about, but something was happening to me. I wanted more. This type of dialogue stirred my mind and spirit. There was a new desire to dig into God's Word. Something was taking place in my spirit. I felt I had to learn as much as I could about God's Word.

That happened over 50 years ago. Through all these years I have developed an insatiable desire to study God's Word. I have studied, preached, taught, meditated, and now love it because, the Bible points me and others to Jesus. The Bible is full of words. There are amazing words that Jesus Himself shared with us. Some of them are well known while others are not as familiar.

Words.

Yes, the words of Jesus. This book is a small result of my journey to study and learn the words of Jesus. These words change lives. I am one that has been changed.

Jesus often says the unusual. In this book, Words That Changed History, a father and son take a look at some of the unique words of Jesus to unravel his greatest teachings. These are the words that have changed history. Despite being two thousand years old, they continue to impact lives today. People who have read those words have found their entire world turned upside down.

This book is the result of a father and son's dialogue over the period of many years. We both have decided to dedicate our lives to the serious study of Scripture, and as a result we have had many debates over the meaning of certain passages. These conversations have taken place around the kitchen table, at coffee shops, in meeting rooms, and stretched late into the evening as we both sat in the living room debating. In most of these conversations both of us assume we are correct in our interpretation.

It is important as you read this book to realize that we are still studying, learning, and being transformed as a result of the words of Jesus. Not only have these words changed history, but they have changed our lives as well. We are but a small part of the worldwide conversation that has been going on for two thousand years about the life and ministry of Jesus.

In this book we want to welcome you to join us on a small part of that journey. When we enter into this dialogue we find ourselves swimming in the stream of conversation that has been going on for thousands of years.

We hope that this book will challenge and encourage you, but most of all we hope that you will be drawn to the Jesus that we have both come to know through the Scriptures. During our many interactions together, we often times disagree, and our discussions are spirited. However, if you were to ask us both what one thing we can both agree on, it would be this: we both are drawn to Jesus. His words have changed both of our lives.

This book has brought us closer together, and we have each learned from the other about how we should understand the meaning of Jesus' powerful words. This book is not meant to be the last word on the subject of Jesus (as if that were even possible). John the apostle tells us that if one were to write down all the words of Jesus, you could fill an entire library with volumes. This book is meant to be the first word in a conversation about what Jesus' words meant. You may find yourself disagreeing with us in some chapters, and we think that is great. In fact, we would love to continue the conversation with you about this book because we both believe that we are on a journey towards greater understanding, and good conversation is the fuel that propels that journey. You will find our personal email addresses listed below. If you find yourself agreeing, disagreeing, angry, perplexed, confused, or just want to drop us a line and say hello, we would love to hear from you.

These words have changed history, and we hope they will change you too.

Welcome to the conversation.

Dino Pedrone
dinopedrone@gmail.com

Jonathan Pedrone
jonathanpedrone@gmail.com

BEGINNING

"In the beginning God created the heavens and the earth."
--Genesis 1:1

"In the beginning was the Word and the Word was with God and the Word was God."
--John 1:1

I (DINO) WAS RELAXING IN AN EASY CHAIR IN THE PASTOR'S OFFICE WAITING to go to the platform to deliver the Sunday morning message. Numerous congregants were walking by the room to go to the church service. As they walked past the office, I could hear a few bits of various conversations. "How are the kids?" "Did you get the job?" "I hear we have a guest speaker here today." Then a little innocent boy who appeared to be 5 or 6 years old asked his father and mother "Who made God?" "Shh!" was the mother's reply as she dragged him along. Perhaps this was not the time to deal with this, but what a great question! I assumed that something was said in Sunday school to peak this youngster's question.

Brilliant men and women have posed this question. For example, Bertrand Russel, born May 18, 1872, was a philosopher, historian, political activist, and Nobel laureate. Russell, who lived nearly 100 years, was the author of more than 70 books. One of his best-remembered quotes is: "I would never die for my beliefs because I might be wrong", and "The only thing that will redeem mankind is cooperation."[3] Russell was also a mathematician, social critic, and avid writer. As one reads his writings it does not take long to know he is not a Christian and his authority is not from Scripture. His scientific studies do not make room for God and he would not be the person I would choose to answer the lad's question.

---

[3] Lyons, Leonard. "The Lyons Den." *New York Times*, June 23, 1964. Accessed April 5, 2019.

There are other such individuals who are separated by centuries with the same brilliance and yet question, as this young boy did, about God. Men like Aristotle, Ludwig Wittgenstein, Immanuel Kant, Stephen Hawking, and dozens of other scholars too have struggled with the boys question, "Who made God?" For example, Hawking, in an interview with *El Mundo* in 2014 said, "Before we understand science, it is natural, to believe that God created the universe. But now science offers a more convincing explanation. What I meant by 'we would know the mind of God' is we would know everything that God would know, if there were a God, which there isn't. I am an atheist."[4] Hawking also said, "One can't prove that God doesn't exist. But science makes God unnecessary"[5]

The young child's question is very relevant and needs explanation. Perhaps the parents dealt with the answer over lunch after church. Being a parent, I am very familiar with such questions by children at the most inappropriate times. I did the same with my parents. It is a habit all children seem to acquire.

Genesis 1:1 sets the stage for the Biblical narrative. The word "beginning" is appropriately used at the start of the story. The start of creation is the heart of the early pages of Scripture. It is interesting to notice that God created all things, but He did not create Himself. There are seven days of creation, but on none of those days is it said that God was created. From the very beginning it is assumed that He is. If God were created, He no longer is God because He would not be the origin of all things.

We may often find ourselves saying things like, (God would never do that). Then we list something that we think He wouldn't do. Suffering, death, persecution, and numerous other maladies are blamed on God. We all want a God who does things to our liking so that we can respond 'Everyone lived happily ever after.' There is a God we want. He is not,

---

[4] Johnston, Lori. "'I'm Not Afraid': What Stephen Hawking Said about God, His Atheism and His Own Death." The Washington Post. March 14, 2018. Accessed April 05, 2019. https://www.washingtonpost.com/news/acts-of-faith/wp/2018/03/14/im-not-afraid-what-stephen-hawking-said-about-god-his-atheism-and-his-own-death/?utm_term=.5cdba842c262.

[5] Watt, Nick. "Stephen Hawking: 'Science Makes God Unnecessary'." ABC News. September 7, 2010. Accessed April 05, 2019. https://abcnews.go.com/GMA/stephen-hawking-science-makes-god-unnecessary/story?id=11571150.

however, the God who is. If God is God, He can do whatever it is He would want to do. His character is from His person and therefore He is God.

I often hear people say that they have a tough time with the God of the Old Testament. Our attitude of the God of the Old Testament makes little difference with who He is. He is God. He does as He pleases. For example, in the Old Testament God states that He loves Israel because He has chosen to love them. We may cry out and say that this does not seem fair. Stop and think. Who are we to question God? He has every right to do as He pleases. He is God.

There are four concepts that are fundamental to science. "It is almost taken for granted that everything from physics to biology, including the mind, ultimately comes down to four fundamental concepts: matter and energy interacting in an arena of space and time."[6] The opening verse of Genesis introduces us to these fundamental scientific concepts.

"In the beginning" speaks to time. The beginning is the creation of time as we know it today. God has always been. If He had a beginning, He would not be God.

A Hebrew word for God is *Elohim*. *Elohim* is known as the God who is all-powerful who shows by His works that He is in charge of all things. He is creator, sustainer, sovereign, and Lord.

Proverbs 8 speaks of the wisdom of God and seems to be a portrayal of Jesus in the Old Testament. "*The LORD brought me forth as the first of his works, before his deeds of old; I was formed long ages ago, at the very beginning, when the world came to be.*" (Proverbs 8:22, 23). A large section of this chapter of the Proverbs describes the issue that there is no time limit with God. He is forever, and everything is in the eternal now for Him.

> "*Jesus Christ is the same yesterday, today, and forever.*" (Hebrews 13:8).

The word "*created*" speaks to energy. There are two Hebrew words that are used interchangeably in scripture. These words help us answer

[6] Johnson, George. "Beyond Energy, Matter, Time and Space." *New York Times*, January 21, 2014. Accessed April 5, 2019. https://www.nytimes.com/2014/07/22/science/beyond-energy-matter-time-and-space.html.

the question as to whether God made all things from something or without anything. The fact is both words speak to the instantaneous act of God. One Hebrew word is *bara* which sometimes refers to create while the word *asah* has reference to making or doing something.

There are many examples of these two words interchangeable teaching. In Genesis 1:2 the reference is to create *bara* in addressing the heavens and the earth. In Genesis 1:7 *asah* refers to the expanse between the waters that are above and below. In Genesis 2:3, 4 *bara* is used to describe the fact that God created all that exists. A*sah* is used in Genesis 2:3, 4 for the creation the heaven and earth. "The context of Genesis, indeed the whole Bible, is overwhelming in favor of interpreting both *bara* and *asah* in Genesis 1 as virtuously instantaneous acts."[7]

This is energy. God created the entire cosmos as an instantaneous act. God spoke and as Genesis 1 teaches, 'It was so'. Powerful and magnificent energy from God brought this into existence.

Space is referred to by the word heavens. What an amazing universe of the heavens is above us, our Milky Way Galaxy has many star formations in nebulae. A galaxy consists of stars and other objects plus nebulae with interstellar mediums of gas and dark holes. There are billions of stars, and to reach one is unlikely. "The closest star to Earth is Proxima Centauri, located 4.2 light years away. In other words, it takes light itself more than 4 years to complete the journey from Earth. If you tried to hitch a ride on the fastest spacecraft ever launched from Earth, it would still take you more than 70,000 years to get there from here."[8]

There are about 10 billion galaxies in the observable universe. Perhaps we should stop here and recommend that you, our reader, take a moment to consider the vast expanse of the universe. It is almost too much to comprehend, and yet God is the one who created all of this. The heavens are a remarkable space that God has made. When the Psalmist wrote, *"The heavens declare the glory of God"* (Psalm 19:1a) he wrote

---

[7] Mortenson, Terry. "Did God Create (bara) or Make (asah) in Genesis 1?" Answers in Genesis. August 15, 2007. Accessed April 05, 2019. https://answersingenesis.org/genesis/did-god-create-bara-or-make-asah-in-genesis-1/.

[8] Cain, Fraser. "Interesting Facts About Stars." Universe Today. May 04, 2017. Accessed April 05, 2019. https://www.universetoday.com/25145/interesting-facts-about-stars/.

great truth about the creator. When we think of this grandeur we realize that this is the work of Elohim God.

"Matter" is declared in the word Earth. The earth is larger than Pluto, Mercury, and Mars. The circumference around the equator is 24,901 miles. When the earth is measured using the meridional circumference meaning the flattening of the poles it is 24,860 miles. The earth is the third planet from the sun and the only one of the three that shows life. The earth is big, although not nearly as big as the universe. The scriptures begin with a declaration that this all came about because of Elohim God.

Let's return to our little friend's question. Who made God? I wondered about that when I was a child. Small children can believe in many things from wizards to demons and angels. Parents and those who love them are very impressionable on children. Children need to know that if someone made God then He isn't God. As a child grows up there are challenges because they learn that not everyone can be trusted. It is here that loving parents and focused teachers can share the story of creation and in terms that a child can understand be told that time, energy, matter and space are the result of a God who spoke all things into existence.

This brings us to John's remarkable statement in John 1:1 about Jesus. John begins his book with a retelling of the creation story:

> *"In the beginning God created the heavens and the earth"* (Genesis 1:1)
>
> *"In the beginning was the Word, and the Word was with God, and the Word was God."* (John 1:1)

John purposefully echoes the story of Genesis 1 at the beginning of his book to make a startling claim. That at the beginning of the world, when all things were brought into existence by God, at the formation of galaxies, the Word was there with God in the creative process. And who is this "word"? John goes on to tell us in John 1:14: *"The Word became flesh and made his dwelling among us."*

The book of John was originally written in Greek. The Greeks used the term word to mean not only the spoken word, but also the unspoken word. They used this term to refer to reason, the rational process that governs everything in the universe. "The Stoics, a group of philosophers in the third century B.C. spoke of logos as the mind and purpose of God that permeated creation."[9] If we were to ask someone from this ancient civilization what the term word meant, they would understand it to be the very substance that makes up the entire universe, the underlying principle of all things.

The Jews also used the term word to refer the foundational substance of the universe, but for them the word was a reference not to rationality, but to God, because God is the one who has created all things. When John says that the Word was with God in the beginning, he is appealing to both his Jewish and Greek audience, using a term they would both be familiar with. The Word is not simply just rationality, the substance of all our thoughts. The Word is not only Elohim who created all things by speaking them into existence. The Word is Jesus.

We might not think of Jesus as being present in the beginning of time. When we read the word, beginning we might not think of Jesus. We might assume that He only came into existence two thousand years ago in a small town in Israel. But John tells us that Jesus, like God has no beginning. He is the Word, and He is God. He was there from the beginning.

Who made God? He has always been. He is the source of all things, and He holds all things together. When Jesus said that He and His father were one, it is a reminder that God not only created all things, but that He loved us enough to come down and dwell amongst us. Jesus was there at the beginning, loved us enough to come down and dwell among us, and remains with us to this day.

---

[9] Hamilton, Adam. *John: The Gospel of Light and Life*. Nashville, TN: Abingdon Press, 2015. 16.

LEGEND

"Jesus was not just an identikit figure pasted together from the Old Testament. He transcended and transformed the ancient models. He filled them with fresh meaning in relation to his own unique person, his example, teaching and experience of God."[10]
Christopher J. Wright

"Hosanna to the Son of David"
Matthew 21:9

You have 30 seconds.

30 seconds to run into your house and save one item before everything in your home is completely destroyed. You can only save physical objects, all of your loved ones have already been rescued so your purpose is to choose the possession in your home that you love the most. What would you save? This type of hypothetical scenario is meant to help us discern what the most important objects in our life are.

When I (Jonathan) was a teenager my grandmother passed away, and after her death we were cleaning out a closet underneath the stairs of my boyhood home. In the back of that closet I found a bat, and immediately assumed it was just an ordinary bat until I looked closer. I found scrawled in blue pen the name "Babe Ruth". I assumed the bat was a cheap imitation, until later I found a telegram from 1924 folded in a book my grandmother owned addressed to my grandfather. In short choppy (and incorrect) telegram style the telegram said "*You have won a Babe Ruth prize please bring picture yourself to me early Thursday morning.*"

If I were presented with this scenario I know exactly what I would

[10] Wright, Christopher J. H. *Knowing Jesus through the Old Testament*. Downers Grove, Ill: InterVarsity Press, 1996. 117.

rush into the house to save. In my living room I have that baseball bat in a custom bat frame. Babe Ruth was one of the greatest players in baseball history. When he retired he had blasted 714 home runs, a record that would stand from 1935 until 1974. Today, baseball fans debate whether or not anyone in the last one hundred years can come close to Ruth's prowess on the baseball diamond. If you were to ask me today who the greatest baseball player in history was I would immediately respond with Babe Ruth. Even though I never saw him play in a single game, in my mind Babe Ruth is the greatest player ever to play the game. He transcends all other players in the sport. In short, Babe Ruth is an American legend.

One of the first questions I receive when someone sees the bat hanging on my wall is "what is that bat worth?" The assumption is that because Babe Ruth is such a great baseball player, and because he passed away over 60 years ago there must be great value in my relic. The truth of the matter is I have no idea what the bat is worth. I have never taken it to be examined by a sports collector. I have not for a moment considered selling the bat to one of the many fans out there who would love a chance to own a piece of baseball history. The reason I have never even given a moment's thought to parting with my bat is because of who that bat is from. My grandfather.

My grandfather died before I was born, but he lives on in fantastic stories told by my family members. When I am with family members who are older than me, and were able to spend time with my grandfather, I love to listen to their stories about the great man that he was. The stories that surround him are certainly partly apocryphal, because as these tales have been told time and time again they always grow and expand. My grandfather has now become bigger than life in my mind because of these stories. When I think of my last name, and my family history, my grandfather is who I think about. Even though I have never met him, I would love for someone to tell me that I remind them of Fred Pedrone. If you asked the average person who they first want to meet in heaven, they may respond that their first stop would be with Jesus, or maybe one of the apostles. Personally, my first stop will be to sit with my grandfather, and to ask him about the baseball bat, and quite possibly debate who the greatest player of all time is.

This brings us to the gospel of Matthew, whose author tells us a legendary story right at the beginning. When the Gospel author, Matthew, decides to tell the story of Jesus, he begins by giving his readers a brief history of the family of Jesus. For modern readers Matthew begins his Gospel in the most boring way possible, a genealogy.

The Old Testament is comprised of 39 books of varying lengths. Many Christians at the start of a new year make a commitment to read through the entire Bible in a year, which is not an easy task. Like most New Year's resolutions keeping the commitment to read through the entire Bible lasts about two weeks, or until you hit the genealogical records in the Old Testament. The story of creation is exciting, and Abraham had a very interesting life, but when you get to *"the sons of Eliphaz: Teman, Omar, Zepho, Gatam and Kenaz"* (Genesis 36:11), you can be forgiven for skimming through the next few pages.

Matthew begins his Gospel in a very similar way.

> *"A record of the genealogy of Jesus Christ the son of David, the son of Abraham"* (Matthew 1:1).

At the very outset Matthew points us to the family of Jesus through a genealogy. Matthew wants us to know that his ancestors matter because much like my baseball bat, something has been passed down to Jesus from those who came before him.

Matthew tells us that Jesus is the son of David. David is a legendary figure in the Old Testament scriptures. Many are familiar with the story of David and Goliath in the book of 1 Samuel. David, a small insignificant shepherd, is sent into battle against the greatest warrior in the ancient world. Not only is David completely outmatched in size and strength but he goes into battle without any of the armor common for the day. David enters into battle with only a few small stones and slingshot. Imagine today going into battle against Seal Team Six armed with a Super Soaker and some water balloons. Miraculously David is able to defeat the giant Goliath and so the legend of David is born.

The prophet Samuel anoints David king over Israel. The only problem with this anointing is that there already is a king over Israel and David is not in the line of succession. In fact, the current king of Israel Saul has quite a jealous streak. After David kills the giant Goliath he cuts off his head, not to ensure that Goliath is dead, but rather to take the head as a trophy. Imagine a young boy walking through the streets of Israel carrying the severed head of what was the strongest, most feared warrior of the ancient world. 1 Samuel 17:54 tells us that David kept the head later bringing it to Jerusalem. If you walked into David's house, there on the mantle was the skull of his great enemy. Not a trophy that you could easily ignore.

David's status as a hero grows quickly. After his defeat and decapitation of the great warrior Goliath, the people of Israel sing a song praising both Saul and David. *"Saul has slain his thousands and David his tens of thousands"* (I Samuel 18:7). In the Ancient Near East, exaggeration of military victory was often utilized to show that you were greater than all of your enemies, and David was the greatest victor of them all. While the people sang the praises of King Saul, they were even more impressed with David. This was certainly not the type of song a jealous Saul wanted to hear from his people.

If we were in the situation that Saul found himself in, we may respond in a similar way. Saul had every reason to be jealous and concerned. In the ancient world you were king until someone stronger or with more military might was able to defeat or kill you. 1 Samuel 18:12 tells us that Saul was afraid of David because of his great success. Saul needs to find a way to ensnare David so that he will be defeated and so that Saul can hold onto his throne. So Saul does what any of us would do, he offers David his daughter Michal in marriage.

But in giving his daughters hand in marriage Saul has an ulterior motive, and a simple request. Saul proposes a very simple dowry for David to pay. *"Say to David, the king wants no other price for the bride than a hundred Philistine foreskins"* (1 Samuel 18:24). A hundred foreskins… let that sink in for a moment.

David seems undaunted by this request (because when you are in love, what are a few hundred foreskins to stand in the way)? Saul is sure that David will fail in his attempt, and Saul's jealousy will be satiated with the death of David as he attempts to retrieve this unusual dowry.

If killing Goliath and keeping his severed head as a trophy was not enough, David goes out and kills not one hundred Philistines, but two hundred Philistines. Saul sends David on a suicide mission and David comes back stronger than ever.

And what happens next? *"He brought their foreskins and presented the full number to the king so that he might become the kings son-in-law"* (1 Samuel 18:27). David has a sack of two hundred dead Philistines foreskins and he makes a show of bringing them before the king to count them out one by one. One, two, three, four, five... imagine what was going through Saul's mind as David pulled out foreskin after foreskin out of a bag and proceeded to count them out one by one.

At this point Saul should have seen the writing on the wall. A man willing to collect two hundred foreskins from his enemy is definitely a warrior that you want nothing to do with. It also begs the question, were the Philistines alive or dead when David removed their foreskins?

David proceeds to become king over Israel and is revered as one of the greatest kings in their history.

David's legendary status comes with a dark side as well. Despite his miraculous military victories and his meteoric rise to king, David fell short. David desired to build a temple, which would act as a dwelling place for God on earth. However, he was unable to build the temple because David was also an adulterer and murderer; two sins which kept him from truly becoming the greatest king in Israel's history. In fact, despite David's auspicious beginnings over time his kingdom falls apart, his own family revolts against him trying to steal the throne from him, similar to the way that the kingdom was ripped from Saul.

When Matthew opens his book saying that Jesus is in the line of David, this is a small part of the story that would come to the first audiences mind. David, a man who could defeat giants, a man who would carry around a bag containing the foreskins of his enemies, a man who was the head of a violent military campaign that ended with David setting up his kingdom in the city of Jerusalem (2 Samuel 5).

Matthew begins his gospel with a genealogy, a sure fire way to put readers to sleep, or to cause them to skip down the page until the real story begins. But with the words *"Jesus Christ the son of David"* Matthew wants us to imagine a revolutionary figure in the mold of David.

In Matthew 22 when Jesus asks the Pharisees who the Messiah's ancestors will be they immediately respond *"the son of David"* (Matthew 22:42). A new Davidic king would come who would defeat his enemies with the sword. When Matthew mentions the name of David, a whole host of expectations would come along with that reference. Matthew is invoking the name of one of the greatest kings in history, and at the same time saying the story of Jesus' life will be as great as the story of David.

For Matthew Jesus transcends David. But, how is Jesus different than David?

Jesus does not seek political or military strength. In Samuel 5, David marches into Jerusalem which was at the time populated by the Jebusites. Clearly this group of people had not heard of David's conquests because they deride David by saying, *"you will not get in here; even the blind and the lame can ward you off"* (2 Samuel 5:6). Their hubris was short lived, as the very next verse tells us that *"David captured the fortress of Zion, the City of David."* The Old Testament authors refer to it not as the city of Jerusalem, but the city of David. His status had grown to the extent that cities were now named after him.

We may expect Jesus to act in the same way, but in Matthew's Gospel Jesus is decidedly different from David. In Matthew 21 Jesus comes into Jerusalem, not as a conquering king, but riding on a donkey. David enters the city as a conqueror taking it from his enemies. Jesus enters the city, not on a horse in full splendor, but on a donkey. As he makes his way through the streets the people's response is to chant *"Hosanna to the Son of David"* (21:9). The people of Jerusalem remember the legend of David and his conquest, and assume that this Jesus will establish his kingdom in the same way that David did, through sheer brute strength. Jesus will not fall prey to the myth that the person with the most political or military power can change the world. Instead Jesus comes into Jerusalem as a servant.

Jesus enters the city of Jerusalem only to be killed there a week later as a common criminal by the enemies of the state. Jesus is not triumphant by exercising great violence and power; instead Jesus is defeated on a cross. The people wanted a new legendary figure to save them, what they received was a humble servant who could not save his own life at the hands of his enemies. Maybe this Jesus we meet in the gospels is not like David at all, but rather a better version of David.

Christians sometimes think that if they could just elect the right President, if they could just win the next legislative battle and establish morality in America through laws; we could finally win a Davidic victory. Jesus instead gives us a model that shuns this type of power, showing us that the way of humility is the way to truly change the world.

Jesus will enter Jerusalem not with great might and power, but with love and compassion. He is willing to give up all of his power, even to the point of death. David may have conquered Jerusalem for a short time, but Jesus changes the entire world through his sacrifice.

As Jesus prepares to make the ultimate sacrifice, the disciples assume that after Jesus' entrance in Jerusalem that he will play the role of the new Davidic king and conquer by the sword. Before He is crucified Jesus goes into a garden to pray. While in the garden Judas, one of his disciples who had betrayed him, leads a contingent of soldiers to violently arrest Jesus. The disciple's first thoughts are to violently defend their king. Much like the ancient story of David, they assume the battle will now begin with swords drawn and bloodshed. *"One of Jesus' companions reached for his sword, drew it out and struck the servant of the high priest, cutting off his ear"* (Matthew 26:51). The way of David is to cut off the heads and ears of your opponents; the way of Jesus however looks much different. *"Put your sword back in its place, for all who draw the sword will die by the sword... Am I leading a rebellion that you have come out with swords and clubs to capture me?"* (Matthew 26:52-55).

The way of Jesus is not the way of David. The Jesus we meet today is not a warrior of violence, but a Prince of Peace. If we are to follow the way of Jesus we must do so not by gaining more might, status, prestige or power, but instead we follow Him by giving up the power that our world so ardently craves. It is by giving up power that we live in the way of Jesus.

My baseball bat represents a line to my grandfather and my past. When I look at the bat that hangs on my wall I am reminded of where I came from, and I reflect on the legendary stories that are told about my grandfather. I would like nothing better to be remembered like my grandfather is remembered by those who survive him.

Matthew begins his story telling us that Jesus is a descendent of David. The story of David is one of violence, coercion, and conquest. The story of Jesus however will be one of service, inclusion, and love. Jesus will be remembered as coming from the line of David, but Jesus will not be like David.

Legend, a word we might not associate with Jesus from his genealogy, but it is a word that certainly came to mind when Matthew sat down to write his anthology of the life of Jesus.

BIRTHDAY

"The birthday of the most divine is ... the day which we might justly set on par with the beginning of everything, in that he restored order when everything was disintegrating and falling into chaos and gave a new look to the whole world. All the communities should have one same New Year's Day, the birthday of the most divine Caesar." [11]
--Marcus J. Borg

"And there were shepherds living out in the fields nearby, keeping watch over their flocks at night."
--Luke 2:8

INVITATIONS, BALLOONS, CAKE, BANNERS, CARDS, PLATES, TABLECLOTH, streamers, and don't forget to pick up the food.

My wife Karen and I (Jonathan) recently celebrated the first birthday of our son William, and like many parents we went all out for his birthday party. We had everything for a wonderfully themed first birthday, even a special outfit for William to wear while he dug into his very first birthday cake. It was a festive time to celebrate our son's birthday. Family and friends came to help us honor William on this important day, culminating with the opening of what seemed at the time to be an endless amount of toys. Our living room was covered in more toys than William knew what to do with. Like most kids, he spent the afternoon playing with the boxes that the toys came in.

Despite the good time had by all, I couldn't help but think critically about this party. William enjoyed his cake, and I am sure he was happy to see all of his grandparents together, but the reality is that he will not likely remember his first birthday party when he is older. Can you

[11] Borg, Marcus J. *Jesus: Uncovering the Life, Teachings, and Relevance of a Religious Revolutionary.* San Francisco: Harper San Francisco, 2006. 67.

remember when you turned one? Was there a party or cake? Did you like the flavor of the cake? Do you remember what presents were piled up on the table for you to open? A better question might be if you can remember your last birthday celebration, the type of cake that was eaten, and what you were given as a gift. If you were to ask me that question, I would honestly struggle to remember. Birthdays are important moments in our lives. They are an opportunity to spend time with those who mean the most to you, and they are the one day of the year where you are the complete center of attention.

At times I joke with my wife that the entire birthday party tradition is a scam. We can easily spend hundreds of dollars on a party not really for the person of honor, but rather on trying to impress others. The expectations that come with the celebration can at times drive us to go to ridiculous lengths to have the biggest and best party. Your friends had a bounce house for their child, so this year you go all out and have pony rides. The competition to impress our friends and family can sometimes become the focal point of the celebration.

It is equally interesting that every October when my birthday comes around, my attitude immediately changes, and I anticipate my celebration. In a way that can only be described as selfish, my attitude towards the expenses of a birthday celebration immediately change, and suddenly custom cakes, balloons, and gifts are all worth it because I am the recipient.

Birthdays are important moments in our lives because they mark out another year of life accomplished. Whether it is my son turning one or a grandfather entering a new decade of life, we celebrate the day of our birth. In the ancient world, the day of a leader's birth was equally important. An inscription from the ancient city of Halicarnassus in Caria, which is in modern day Turkey describes the birth of Caesar Augustus:

> *"Since the eternal and immortal nature of everything has bestowed upon mankind the greatest good with extraordinary benefactions by bringing Caesar Augustus in our blessed time the father of his own country, divine Rome, and ancestral Zeus, savior of the common race of men, whose providence has not only fulfilled but actually*

> *exceeded the prayers of all. For land and sea are at peace and cities flourish with good order, concord and prosperity."*[12]

Imagine a birthday invitation with the line "come and celebrate the birth of our son who as a result of his birth has brought peace to all nations and has saved all men from calamity." An invitation like that certainly would require an expensive party. Good luck finding the perfect gift for the person that has saved the entire world and brought about world peace simply by being born.

What would a guest list for a person like this look like? What dignitaries, politicians, world leaders, and celebrities would be worthy of an invitation? The guest list would be carefully guarded, and security would be tight. Getting beyond that velvet rope into the party for the person who has saved the entire world would certainly be difficult. It would be the hottest ticket on earth, the most exclusive party, the must attend event of the year.

This type of sentiment was common in the first century when making a reference to the leaders of the day. The Caesars would make grand claims about themselves in order to bolster the legitimacy of their reign. This practice goes back thousands of years, even to the ancient Egyptians whose leaders were said to be representative of the gods who ruled the entire world. The birthdate of these rulers was considered the starting point of all history. In fact, several ancient rulers demanded that the calendar be amended so that the first day of the first year is the date of their birth. In this time, birthdays were even more important than they are for us today.

Luke begins Jesus' birth story with a specific reference to Caesar Augustus (Luke 2:1; 3:1). Luke is the only one of the Gospel writers to mention the name of the ruling Caesar. The reference to Augustus would bring the claims of the Roman Rulers to anyone reading Jesus' infancy story. They would immediately recognize that Luke is calling to the forefront the birth of Augustus (which means "divine favor"). A new king is being born, but this king will not be like the other rulers of

[12] Borg, Marcus J., and John Dominic Crossan. *The First Christmas: What the Gospels Really Teach about Jesus's Birth.* New York: Harper One, 2007. 156.

the day. His birthday will be celebrated for thousands of years to come, but He will not come with fanfare and grand claims. The calendar will one day be organized around His birth so that every time anyone writes the date they are recognizing the importance of this day. But this king will not be like the other kings, His first birthday will be quite different.

In the nativity story in the book of Luke, the invitees to the birth of Jesus were not dignitaries, important politicians, business leaders, or even individuals that the parents knew. Luke tells us that *"there were shepherds living out in the fields nearby, keeping watch over their flocks at night"* (Luke 2:8). Imagine a birthday party for your son or daughter where those who show up to celebrate are complete strangers. Even worse, those strangers are not the type of people that you would invite into your house in the first place.

Those who are familiar with the story of the Scripture should immediately recognize the reference here. We know that Jesus was born in the line of David, who was assigned the task of working as a shepherd (1 Samuel 16:11). One of the most famous Psalms portrays God as a good shepherd who keeps watch over the sheep in His care (Psalm 23). So why does Luke go out of his way to tell us that shepherds came to visit Jesus on the night of His birth? For that answer we need to understand a little more about the world into which Jesus was born.

The vocation of being a shepherd has been around for thousands of years and was an important part of the economy in Jesus' day. In Genesis 4 we are told that Abel brought a sacrifice to God from his flocks. The life of a shepherd was a lonely one because the flocks needed a large space to graze. This meant that as civilization developed with people increasingly finding life in a community as safer and more satisfying, the community still needed those who would sacrifice their membership in the community to work in the wilderness with the flocks.

A shepherd was also a defender because in the wild there was the constant threat; animals trying to pick off one of the flock (1 Samuel 17:34-36). This life of isolation and protection led to a special relationship between the shepherd and his sheep. The gospel of John tells us that a shepherd knew each and every sheep that he would watch over (John 10:14). A close relationship with the flock meant that the majority of a shepherd's time was spent alone and isolated. A shepherd lived a nomadic, lonely lifestyle. If being isolated was not enough, the life of the shepherd was even more difficult because of the economic system in which they lived that pushed them to the lowest rungs of society.

In our society today we recognize three basic social classes: upper, middle, and lower class. These classes resonate with us because we can immediately recognize the class to which we belong. We know where we fit into the social strata of our society. In fact, if you take a moment and think about it, your friends are likely from a very similar social class to you.

This was not the case in the first century. Society was split into two distinct social classes, those who were in the upper class (a very small segment of society) and the much larger lower class. These classes were kept in place by the domination system of the day. The lower class would produce the regular daily needs of society through agriculture and manual work. The upper class knew exactly how much they could extract from the lower class without pushing them so far as to cause a rebellion.[13] The upper class did not produce wealth themselves; instead, they relied on the economic system of domination to keep their place in society. This was done through taxation of agricultural production, personal ownership of most of the land that others worked on, and through slave labor. It is into this social reality that Jesus is born. A person was born into either the upper or lower social class and that is where that person would spend their entire life. Upward social mobility was very rare in the first century.[14]

Within this stratification of society, shepherds would have been at one of the lowest rungs of the social class. They occupied a position in society that was firmly entrenched in the lower class and kept even further from integration into society because of their isolation. A shepherd recognized that they were near the bottom of the totem pole of society. They would be one of the last groups that you would invite to the coronation of a king. Imagine the laughter and ridicule that a dirty, poor shepherd would face showing up to a manor seeking entrance to the extravagant birthday party of a soon to be king.

Luke carefully points out in his birth story the presence of the

---

[13] McLaren, Brian D. *The Voice of Luke: Not Even Sandals: With Devotional Notes throughout.* Nashville, TN: Thomas Nelson, 2007.

[14] Gower, Ralph. *The Manners and Customs of Bible times.* Chicago: Moody Press, 1987.

shepherds in nearby fields. In fact for Luke, they are the sole human witnesses to the birth of Jesus outside of the immediate family. Luke also writes that Jesus is born in the town of David (Bethlehem). This is a clear indication that Luke wants his readers to remember the humble beginning of David as a shepherd (1 Samuel 16), who would rise one day to be one of the greatest kings over all of Israel. David goes from the most humble of beginnings to the most powerful man in the kingdom. Luke crafts a story that tells us that Jesus will follow a similar pattern.

Unlike the birth of a Caesar, where a new proclamation of peace, prosperity and salvation would be proclaimed to all, the birth of Jesus takes place in the most ordinary of places with a strange set of witnesses. There is no grand celebration, no birthday party, and no guest list of important dignitaries; instead, the poor, vagabond, outcast shepherds are invited to the witness the birth of the new King.

For Luke, Jesus' birth is not an announcement that things will remain the way they have always been with those in power keeping the boot of oppression on those who are on the lower rungs of society. Luke references the first witnesses to the birth of Jesus; those who had absolutely no power in society. Luke's visitors were not dignitaries, political powerhouses, or those with the most connections to the ruling class. Instead, Luke's visitors are the humble and poor.

When you are invited to a birthday party as a guest, you never show up empty handed. A gift is purchased in advance as a token of thanks for the invitation and to celebrate the person of honor. The gift is normally proportional to the level of closeness between you and the person of honor. For a close family member or friend, you spend time selecting the perfect gift to show both your appreciation for that person and as a form of celebration. Every hospital has a gift shop specifically for this purpose. When a child is born, you can conveniently stop by the gift shop on the first floor to purchase an appropriate gift. The shepherds who arrived at the birth of Jesus had nothing with them because they had no means to give any sort of gift.

The first witnesses to the birth of Jesus were poor shepherds who occupied the lowest rung of the social class of the day. They spent most of their time in isolation from everyone else. They traded human companionship for time spent with animals. They worked day and night alone, creating a community amongst themselves, but never welcomed into the lives of their fellow laborers.

In Luke's story, the ones invited to witness the birth of Jesus are not those that can give the most extravagant gift, or the ones that can offer connections to higher society. His guests do not have a high social standing. They will not be the center of attention at his party because no one would go out of their way to talk with them. Instead, Luke gives us a party with the outcast and destitute people in society.

Luke is announcing to us that this Jesus does not judge a person based on their social standing. Jesus is not impressed with the amount of money you make or the connections you have. Jesus is not interested in the gift that you bring to the party. Unlike the rulers of the day who would invite only the upper class in society, Jesus instead goes out into the fields to find those who have been excluded from society.

This resonates with us today, thousands of years later, because in society we are still good at separating people into different groups. We spend our time with people from a similar social class. We become jealous of those who occupy a higher standing in society than we do. We work hard in our professions to be able to afford the house with the gated community. This way we can visibly build a wall around our homes so those who don't have the same means as we do are kept at a distance. We have the innate ability to exclude those who are different or who do not meet our standards for fellowship. Whether it is by race, economic status, orientation, or a plethora of other markers, we are a people who excel on limiting our social circle.

When we plan a birthday party today, we can become consumed with making sure the decorations are right, the guest list is complete, and the food is perfect. We even have to worry about the aftermath of the party because thank you notes will need to be sent to everyone who attended. This is not the way of Jesus for Luke. In the Gospel of Luke, Jesus is different. Jesus invites those who cannot bring anything themselves. He makes the first witnesses of Jesus birth, those who the world had forgotten. The shepherds of the first century were those that society had forgotten.

This Jesus seeks out the lost and desolate. Jesus looks for those who are at the end of their rope.

If you think you have nothing to offer Jesus, if you think you are the last person whom Jesus would ever want to meet, if you are the one who has been rejected by others, if you have closed yourself off to others in the community, if you meet these upside down requirements.

Outcasts, these are the people invited to the birthday of Jesus. When we think of those who are closest to Jesus, we likely do not consider them outcasts, but these are the very types of people that Jesus wants at his birthday. If you have ever felt that you were on the lowest rung of society, if you have felt that you didn't fit in with everyone else, if you have been excluded in any way by others, then outcast is a word you may just have applied to yourself. But in the story of Jesus' birthday, that just means you are on the invitation list for the birth of the most important person in history.

You are on the invitation list to witness the birth of a new kind of King.

EXILE

"Herod, who feared lest the great influence John had over the people might put it into his power and inclination to raise a rebellion (for they seemed ready to do anything he should advise), thought it best by putting him to death, to prevent any mischief he might cause, and not bring himself into difficulties, by sparing a man who might make him repent of it when it would be too late."[15]
Josephus

"John's clothes were made of camel's hair, and he had a leather belt around his waist. His food was locusts and wild honey."
--Matthew 3:4

HOW MANY DAYS ARE LEFT?

We can all relate to the idea of looking forward to something. Looking forward is that anticipation of a future event that gets us through the difficult times. Whether it is a vacation, a visit from a close friend, an upcoming marriage, or even your birthday, we all have things we mark down on our calendar and look forward to.

I (Jonathan) spend my days working as a teacher, and if you were to ask me that question during the month of May, I would have an immediate answer. I would instantly know you were referring to the number of days left in the school year before summer break. The final day of school is circled on the calendar, and every morning that the alarm clock goes off is one day closer to the ultimate freedom of summer break.

My wife and I both work as teachers, and we have countdowns in our classrooms at school and at home. Each school day passed lowers the

[15] Josephus, F. (1999). *The New Complete Works of Josephus*. Grand Rapids, MI.: Kregel Publications. 18.5.2.

number on the wall and brings us one step closer to vacation. The month of May becomes a version of an extended New Year's Eve Party where participants count down to zero to inaugurate a new year. As teachers, we long for the day when we can hit the permanent snooze button for two solid months on our alarm clocks.

All of us can relate in some ways to these seasons of anticipation. We all have seasons of life and anticipate upcoming events. If you attend a liturgical church, the official church calendar grounds participants in the different seasons of worship. We move from weeks celebrating the Epiphany to a time of sacrifice in the days of Lent, to an explosion of celebration of Easter in spring. The fall months bring us looking forward to the arrival of Advent and the celebration of the birth of Jesus. As human beings we are wired around this very sort of anticipation.

The gospel of Mark begins in a most interesting way. Instead of building excitement and building towards a climax, Mark's book begins with the statement: *"The beginning of the gospel about Jesus Christ, the Son of God"* (Mark 1:1).

Mark locates the climax of his entire story in the first line by using a few important terms that first century readers would immediately recognize. First, he writes that this is the beginning of the gospel. The gospel literally means "good news," and many Christians would immediately recognize the gospel as the story of Jesus and his birth, death, and resurrection. However, for the first century audience, the term gospel had not yet been given that connotation. The good news in the first century was a term used primarily of a grand pronouncement from a person in power. When a new ruler would ascend to the throne (it was common in ancient history that rulers would be replaced either through assassination, military defeat, or simply natural death), they would send out the good news to the people that a new era of peace, tranquility, and safety has come about because of their impending reign. The world would be ushered into a new era of peace and prosperity because the new ruler would fix all the problems of the world. The gospel or good news had overtones of a new ruler on the scene. This is in part the reason for Herod's consternation when he hears of a new King of the Jews to be born in Bethlehem (Matthew 2:3-4). A royal pronouncement of a new ruler ascending to the throne was a serious challenge to Herod himself. In America we could relate this to the inauguration of a new President every four years. On January 20th the gospel goes out into the entire world proclaiming a new era of prosperity, jobs, and safety for citizens.

The second important word here is the use of the term "Christ." We can sometimes incorrectly think of the term as a sort of last name for Jesus, the same way that we differentiate ourselves from others. There are many Jonathan's in the world, so in order to identify myself I have the last name Pedrone. Christ is not the surname of Jesus, but rather a title given to Jesus to identify him as the Anointed one, or the Messiah. At the time Mark wrote his gospel, the Jews of the day were looking for the coming of a Messiah or "Christ."

The declaration that Jesus was the Christ is no simple throwaway line at the beginning of Mark's gospel as a way of introduction. Identifying someone as the Messiah was a serious claim and challenge to the authority of the day. It was not something that you would casually claim about anyone. Reza Aslan has pointed out that in the first century simply saying the words, "this is the Messiah," could be a criminal offense punishable by crucifixion. To say that someone was a Messiah was to conjure up all sorts of pent up feelings of aggression and hope amongst the people of Israel.[16] Some Jews of the day thought the coming Messiah would be a conquering hero who would restore the fortunes of the Jewish people, overthrow their oppressors, and set up a new Davidic type reign. Others thought the Messiah would be a priest who would restore true religion to the nation. Others still perceived the Messiah to be an apocalyptic, conquering soldier who would annihilate almost anything in his path. The Dead Sea Scrolls anticipated two different Messiah's: one that would be a Priest and one that would be a King.[17]

There were as many views of what the Messiah would be as there were groups of religious adherents in the first century. One thing we can be sure of is that there is no monolithic view of the Messiah in the first century, but for many passages like Isaiah 11 would have been foundational.

---

[16] Aslan, Reza. *Zealot the Life and Times of Jesus of Nazareth.* New York: Random House, 2013.

[17] Wright, N. T. *Mark for Everyone.* Louisville, KY: Westminster John Knox Press, 2004.

> *"A shoot will come up from the stump of Jesse; from his roots a Branch will bear fruit. The Spirit of the Lord will rest on him – the spirit of wisdom and of understanding, the Spirit of counsel and of power, the Spirit of knowledge and of the fear of the LORD – and he will delight in the fear of the LORD. He will not judge by what he sees with his eyes, or decide by what he hears with his ears; but with righteousness he will judge the needy, with justice he will give decisions for the poor of the earth. He will strike the earth with the rod of his mouth; with the breath of his lips he will slay the wicked"* (Isaiah 11:1-4).

The term "Christ" here is Mark's way of giving us the climax of the story of Jesus at the very beginning of his book. This story of Jesus will be about a new age of history, an age where the Messiah has come in the person of Jesus. Mark is indicating to us that the Messiah has indeed come, and has been embodied in the life and ministry of Jesus. The one that his readers have been waiting in anticipation for, the one that they have had circled on their calendar has finally come. The people of Israel had circled their calendar anticipating the arrival of a new king who would be anointed by God for a specific purpose (Luke 2:29-32). But as we have seen thus far in this book, this Messiah will not be what they had anticipated because the Messiah found in the person and work of Jesus is different than anyone had imagined it would be.

After a dense and impactful introduction, Mark then introduces another character, one familiar to us, but in many ways, one that we may have misunderstood entirely. John the Baptist appears on the scene as promised by the prophet Isaiah: *"I will send my messenger ahead of you, who will prepare your way -A voice of one calling in the wilderness. Prepare the way for the Lord, make straight paths for him"* (Mark 1:2-3).

Whenever one thinks of John the Baptist, immediately the image of a man in strange clothes with a mangy beard comes to mind, dunking people in the water of the Jordan river (Mark 1:5-6). Baptism has become such a common part of our culture that we immediately recognize it and are not surprised that anyone would take part in a strange religious ritual that demands that you be dunked in a pool of water to somehow be considered pure or right before God. Most of us are familiar with baptism and think nothing more of it than it being a nice religious ceremony (usually followed by a nice reception at a family member or friend's home).

If we were to be invited to be witnesses of a baptism today, we would think very little of the consequences of such an act. In the last few years, my family and I have attended the baptisms of several of our friend's children and have even had the great honor to stand in as god-parents. At no point did my wife or I consider the grand political statement being made at such an event, and we had no fear of repercussions from the ruling political class. A baptism today is a celebration tied to membership of a particular church, a symbol of the death and resurrection of Jesus, or simply a way of publically recognizing that a family would like their child to be brought up in a particular faith.

John's baptism would have been viewed as a far stronger political statement, and anyone who would join in with him in this ceremony would be making a strong statement about both their personal faith and their politics. John is sent to announce a new way of life, a revolution that has been ruminating in the hearts of the Jewish people for hundreds of years. Mark explains to us that this is the time that God will finally remember his people and begins a new work. This is what the Jewish people had circled on their calendars for all of those years. For the nation of Israel, it was not something as simple as a vacation or visit from a close friend, but rather it was the fulfillment of God's promises to them. It was what they had been waiting for.

John begins to baptize in the desert region preaching a baptism of repentance for the forgiveness of sins. At first glance we could assume that baptism was simply a public way of declaring your faith in Jesus and that you have joined a particular church; however, it is so much more. The story Mark is referring to is the great story of Israel's deliverance from Egypt during the exodus. The exodus was the framing story for the people of Israel. In America we trace our roots to great figures in history like George Washington, Benjamin Franklin, James Madison, and Abraham Lincoln. The people of Israel traced their history back to the time of Moses and the great exodus from Egypt.

While we may be familiar with the story of Egypt from the Old Testament book of Exodus, it is important to understand what that story meant for a first century Jew. The Jews looked forward to a Messiah that was to come who would at the very least restore Israel's position in the world. How that was to be accomplished is what led to the variety of views of the Messiah that we mentioned earlier. Would it be through military might, a return to true religion, or an apocalyptic type war that would wipe the earth clean of all of God's enemies? Mark seems to indicate to us that none of these options quite fit exactly what John the Baptist was announcing.

From the time of Israel's captivity in Egypt to the announcement of John the Baptist, the people of Israel viewed themselves as living in a continued version of exile. There were brief moments of time where they were free from their oppressors and their overbearing rule, but as a whole the people of Israel viewed themselves as living in exile, unable to even control the land that God had promised to them via Abraham (Genesis 12:1-3; 15:13-15). This exile was caused not because the people did not adhere to the religious festivals, or system of sacrifices perfectly (Micah 6:6-8). The exile was due to the sin of the people. The pattern for the people of Israel in the Old Testament was one of continuous domination by others and exile. Beginning with the fall of the Northern Kingdom to Assyria (1 Chronicles 5:26) and culminating with the eventual fall of Jerusalem and the Southern Kingdom to Babylon (2 Kings 25:1). By the year 586 BC, both the Northern and Southern Kingdoms of Israel had been decimated by foreign powers, and the temple of Solomon had been completely destroyed (2 Kings 25:9).

With the destruction of the Temple of the Lord, the people of Israel were disconnected from God. Their most holy place of worship lay in ruins never to return to its original splendor, and despite later rebuilding efforts, the temple would never regain its former glory (Ezra 3:12-13). There were brief moments of respite from outside rule, but they were short lived. No one in Israel at the time of Jesus felt that the true exile was truly over. They may have been living in their land, but they were still in spiritual exile. During the time of Jesus, the Temple was actually rebuilt by Herod, who was neither a Jew nor a true believer in the one God. This was a serious offense to the Jewish people: even their most holy place was not under their control and had been built by an outsider.

In order to justify the restoration of the Temple, Herod gave a speech to the people of Israel trying to justify his right to rebuild their most holy place. Herod's primary goal was not restoration of true worship, but rather to build a lasting memorial to himself. He erected great buildings so that his name would be remembered far after his death. Herod told the people:

> *"Since I am now, by God's will, your governor, and I have had peace a long time, and have gained great riches and large revenues, and, what is the principal feeling of all, I am at amity with and well regarded by the Romans, who if I may so say, are the rulers of the whole world, I will try to correct that imperfection* [the current temple was not nearly grand enough], *which has arisen from the necessity of our affairs, and the slavery we have been under formerly, and to make a thankful return, after the most pious manner, to God, for what blessings I have received from him, by giving me this kingdom, and that by rendering his temple as complete as I am able."*[18]

Imagine for a moment the horror of the Jewish people. A non-believer will radically reconstruct their Temple with revenues gained by cooperation with their oppressors. Herod had great power because he was in coordination with the Roman Empire, which had oppressed the nation of Israel through a system of taxation and domination. The Temple would no longer be built to honor God, but as a way of memorializing Herod's life and work.

Where had the Jews gone wrong, and what had caused the exile? It was due to the nation of Israel's apostasy and idolatry. They had turned from the one true God as a community of people and as a result had been punished with exile. When Mark tells us that John's baptism was for repentance and the forgiveness of sins (1:4), he is speaking specifically about the exile that Israel was facing.

> *"If her sin has caused her exile, her forgiveness will mean her national re-establishment. This needs to be emphasized in the strongest possible terms: the most natural meaning of the phrase 'forgiveness of sins' to a first century Jew is*

[18] Josephus. 15.11.1

> *not in the first instance the remission of individual sins, but the putting away of the whole nation's sins. And, since the exile was punishment for those sins, the only sure sign that the sins had been forgiven would be the clear and certain liberation from exile."* [19]

It is within this context of continuing exile that the nation of Israel was in, and in which we must understand John's message and his call for repentance of sin and submission to baptism. This is the point where we can fall prey to an anachronistic reading of the Bible and sin as a whole. For many modern readers, sin is simply our individual failings or the ways that we don't live up to the impossible standard of perfection that God has established. But throughout the Old Testament, sin was ascribed to the people as a whole. Judaism in the first century (of which Jesus was a follower) was not a system of beliefs that if an individual could just get right, they would be made right with God. This type of thinking is pervasive in Christianity today, but this is not what Jesus's message was about. Certainly what you believe is important, and believing the right sorts of things is an outworking of dynamic faith, but for Israel Judaism was a way of life.

John's baptism is not about an individual proclamation that one had accepted Jesus as the promised Messiah and therefore had found a new religious experience that others needed to bear witness to. John's baptism was about the announcing of the end of exile, the breaking through of a new era. It was the announcement of a new king and kingdom and a new way of life. The era of oppression and subjugation was coming to an end. Finally the people would be released from their bondage and forgiven as a nation. God was indeed breaking into the world to do a radical new work.

Mark further drives this point home by describing the place of John's baptism as being in the Jordan River (1:5). The Jordan River runs North and South along the Eastern border of Israel. It flows from the snows of Mount Vernon and ends at the Dead Sea. When the people of Israel left Egypt, they traveled through the Sinai Peninsula in the

---

[19] Wright, N. T. *The New Testament and the People of God.* Minneapolis, MN: Fortress Press, 1994. 273

South. Before entering the new land that was promised to them, they had to cross the Jordan River. This was the final barrier to the people of Israel entering the Promised Land in the Old Testament (Joshua 5). The use of the Jordan River would immediately remind those listening to John's message that just as their forefathers had crossed the river into the promised land of God, so now they too would participate in a ritual re-enacting this ancient crossing. By plunging into the waters via baptism, the people of Israel are reenacting this ancient crossing.

John's baptism was a political statement. Imagine attending a rally whose message was that the current ruling party has had their time in office, but now is the time for the people to take back their power because a new era has begun. The Boston Tea Party of 1773 was a clear act of rebellion against the ruling power of the day. By boarding the ship, the Sons of Liberty were proclaiming to their English rulers that a new day had come, and they would no longer be intimidated or continue to pay the high tax on tea. This is the type of statement that John's baptism makes. The people of Israel are being cleansed both individually and as a nation because the anticipated day had finally arrived.

Immediately Mark makes us aware that Jesus undergoes this baptism as a way of showing the followers of John that indeed the revolution has begun, the exile will soon end, and he is the one who will be leading the people into a new era. Mark likes to use climactic moments in his gospel to frame the entire story. Mark 1:1 is an example of this where he proclaims the gospel is the announcement of Jesus (a new ruler has come) and that this Jesus is indeed the Anointed One, or the Messiah. Mark 1:10-11 is yet another example of a climactic moment in the book. Jesus is baptized by John and *"As Jesus was coming up out of the water, he saw heaven being torn open and the Spirit descending on him like a dove. And a voice came from heaven: 'You are my Son, whom I love; with you I am well pleased.'"* From the beginning of his book until the end, Mark wants us to know that Jesus is the Messiah, the one we have been waiting for. The time that was circled on the calendar has begun in the here and now.

At regular intervals in his book Mark makes similar statements about Jesus:

"... Peter answered, you are the Christ" (Mark 8:29).

> *"Then a cloud appeared and enveloped them, and a voice came from the cloud: 'this is my son, whom I love, listen to him.'"* (Mark 9:7).
>
> *"Again the high priest asked him, 'Are you the Christ [Messiah], the Son of the Blessed One?'"* (Mark 14:61).
>
> *"And when the centurion, who stood there in front of Jesus, heard his cry and saw how he died, he said, 'Surely this man was the Son of God!'"* (Mark 15:39).

Mark carefully places these statements throughout his book to remind us of who Jesus is and what he is going to accomplish. Baptism represents not simply the covering of individual sins and a return to individual piety in seclusion, but a remaking of the entire world. The long exile was finally over, and the people as a whole would be redeemed. The entire community would have their sins forgiven. The baptism of Jesus is a clear marker that this new world is now being inaugurated, and the people have a chance as a community to participate.

If Mark was not clear enough at this point, he continues to drive home the point. After his baptism Jesus is sent into the desert by the Spirit. Immediately after the escape from Egypt, the people of Israel are kept in the desert for 40 years, just as Jesus entered the desert and experienced a temptation lasting 40 days (Mark 1:13). Mark wants us to realize that Jesus is re-animating this exodus story. The replication of the Exodus story in the life of Jesus is a clear indication that God is doing something similar. The people of Israel would understand baptism as a way of showing the world that you were joining into what God was doing. God had freed the nation from the oppression of Egypt hundreds of years earlier and indeed something similar was going to happen in the near future. Participation in baptism for these early followers of John the Baptist was a way of showing their allegiance to the one true God over the ruling empire of the day, and anticipating a fresh work of God in the here and now.

When we participate in the ancient ritual of baptism, we are joining this revolution. We are not simply affirming a set of beliefs or identifying with a particular church, we are joining with others in saying that God is doing something unique in the world, and we want to be a part of that. Movements like this can change the world.

We all look forward to something. For the Jews it was the coming of the Messiah and the new age when their nation and all their people would finally be redeemed. When we participate in the way of Jesus, we are participating not in something as small as personal salvation or individual private piety. When we are baptized or witness the baptism of another, we are saying that God is doing something radical in our world, and we want to be a part of it.

Jesus did not come to just redeem individuals, but the entire world. The purpose of baptism was not a simple public declaration of faith; it was a sign that you were joining the work God is doing in the world. The Baptism of John was not a sign of a new wave of piety overcoming someone. John announced the coming of a new way of life, a way of freedom from oppression, a time where all would be forgiven, and God would radically intervene in the world. As God restored the fortunes of the people of Israel from Egypt, so would God in a new way restore His people from the oppression of the Romans.

Some thought that this would come from a conquering king or marauding soldier who would destroy all the enemies of the people of Israel. But Jesus is not a conquering soldier in fact He will die a humble death. He came instead to release an entire nation from their collective sins and lead them into a new way of life. By participating in John's baptism, you were aligning yourself with an entirely new group of resistance. You were picking up your picket signs and marching through the streets proclaiming that the current way of life is coming to an end, the exile is going to end, and restoration was on the way. When we submit to baptism today, we are not simply proclaiming our private faith to the world or joining a church. Through baptism we have the opportunity to participate in this new revolution, this new way of life.

When we hear the word baptism, we don't normally think of a new revolution that will change the course of history, but for John the Baptist, this is exactly what he was calling people to participate in.

This type of revolution might just be something that we should be counting down to on our calendar.

COAL

"The primary purpose of production is to bless people by producing goods and services that meet the needs of others. That is what loving our neighbors is all about."[20]
--Tony Campolo

"It is more blessed to give than to receive"
--Acts 20:35

I (Dino) recently drove through Miami, Florida, and noticed numerous panhandlers with their signs and requests for funds. I wondered to myself… "If I give to them money will I add to their addictions? Are these legitimate requests?"

I remember a time when I saw firsthand someone was engaged in a scheme to profit from others generosity. I was leading a group on a trip to Israel, and as I boarded a bus in Jerusalem I noticed a blind, crippled man begging. I, along with a few of my fellow pilgrims graciously gave him a few shekels. As our bus slowly pulled away to head to the Dung Gate, I noticed our blind, crippled man quickly gather his things and raced to the gate outpacing our bus. He was a fraud! He was neither blind nor crippled. I immediately wanted my money back. This experience caused me to pause and rethink giving to those who are in similar circumstances; my generosity was taken advantage of.

Most of us know that there are some who claim to be needy, and yet are deceiving us. At the same time there are many who are legitimately in need. We should help them if it is in our power to contribute. There are also times when we find that we are the ones in need. When we find ourselves in need, we may be the ones relying on the help of others.

---

[20] Claiborne, Shane, and Anthony Campolo. *Red Letter Revolution: What If Jesus Really Meant What He Said?* Nashville: Thomas Nelson, 2012. 73.

I was raised by two loving and caring parents. They were very important to others because of their giving hearts. I often saw them give of the little they had to those in need. My father was raised in Italy and came to America. His education was the equivalent of the sixth grade. Mom was a seamstress and my dad developed a dry cleaning business called ABC cleaning. The ABC stood for Always Best Cleaners. They had little money but big hearts. News anchor Tom Brokaw called this generation the greatest generation in part because of their willingness to sacrifice for others. Dad and Mom certainly filled that role.

There was a time, however, when our family was the one in need. In the early 1950's my father came down with pneumonia, and was unable to work for several months. Basic necessities like food were in jeopardy in our home. Another major need was fuel for the house. In the basement of the home there was a bin that was famously called the 'coal bin'. Very quickly it was being depleted of the fuel so necessary to heat the stories of our old Victorian home. One evening we had a visit from a very special person. The pastor of our home church, Dr. Taylor, arrived to pray with our family and check on Dad's health.

Our pastor was a hero to me. I was always in awe of him. Dr. Taylor had a radio ministry that was played daily in our home making him a very familiar voice to our family. In the process of the evening visit he became aware that we had need of coal.

A few days later our home had a visit from the coal company and our bin was full of the much-needed resource that would keep us warm throughout the winter. To our surprise it was a gift from the church. I had always looked up to my pastor before this generous gift, but after this my view of him soared. That happened over 50 years ago and I learned the blessing of receiving when we were in need and it has prompted me to consider learning to give to those in need.

In Acts 20:35 the apostle Paul is addressing the Ephesian elders. They were the leaders of the Ephesian church. He reminds them that in his ministry he coveted money from no one. There were times that Paul the apostle worked with his hands making tents in order to supply resources for ministry and personal needs. Paul spent a great deal of time with the people of Ephesus. He preached for 3 months in the synagogue (Acts 19:8) and two years in the school of Tyrannus (Acts 19:10). During this period Paul did all he could to help the weak. He declares to the elders, *"In everything I did, I showed you that by this kind of hard work we must help the weak, remembering the words the Lord Jesus himself said: 'It is more blessed to give than to receive'"* (Acts 20:35). It is interesting to note that the verb translated weak is addressed to those with bodily weaknesses.

The text tells us that these are the words of the Lord Jesus. However, these words are found nowhere else in sacred scripture. If you were to read through the gospels in their entirety you would not find these words anywhere. We must remember that the words of Jesus in the Bible are those God intended to be there. Jesus said many things that are not recorded in the scriptures. *"Jesus did many other miraculous signs in the presence of his disciples, which are not recorded in this book"* (John 20:30). These beautiful words describe Jesus' view of giving.

Think back in your life. Was there a time when you needed to receive help? Perhaps you felt a little embarrassed because you were viewed as a victim. You may have felt like a victim. It is helpful to remember that your plight allowed someone else to have the privilege of giving. The key to the whole issue of giving is the first word that Jesus gave in these brief words. He used the word blessed.

There are three primary usages of the English word blessed. The common word for blessed is the Greek word *makorizo*. The word carries with it the idea of being satisfied. A blessing then is everything that God provides. The great satisfaction that God provides is found in Jesus alone. Another Greek word for blessed is *eulogeo*.[21] It speaks of good words that we say about others and blessing on our food. The Hebrew word is *'barak'* meaning to praise, salute, congratulate. In each of these instances there is a call to give. The key to all of this is satisfaction. When we learn to give there is deep satisfaction.

Throughout the years that I have been a follower of Jesus Christ I have been learning the joy of giving. My wife and I have given hundreds of thousands of dollars away. Why? I remember the gift of coal and what it meant to us. There was a great feeling of satisfaction for our family. I am also blessed knowing that the church was blessed in giving it. I don't even pretend to have all the answers, but I am learning in my journey

---

[21] Vine, W. E. *Vines Expository Dictionary of Old & New Testament Words*. Nashville, TN: T. Nelson Publishers, 2003.

through life to give. Common sense needs to lead the way. We should pay off our debts, develop an emergency fund, invest for retirement, pay off the mortgage on our house early, prepare for our children's education, and on and on it goes. Despite all these needs it is so satisfying when we give to those who legitimately need it.

Today when I travel by a panhandler I am tempted to look the other way. Some, not all, are deceivers. I must never forget the blessing that came to our humble Italian family when some coal came by our house for the winter. Is there a place you ought to be dropping off some coal? If there is, drop it off, you will find great satisfaction. Remember, it is Jesus who teaches us of the blessing of giving.

Coal is not a word we may associate with Jesus; in fact it is never mentioned in the gospels. However, Jesus recognized that when others are in need we should be meeting those needs. If there are people in our neighborhoods that are in need, Jesus tells us that we should be meeting those needs. Sometimes that means providing coal for a long winter; at other times it might simply be sharing a meal with someone who is lonely. In all things we should be giving sacrificially, because others needs are our needs.

FATHER

"An involved father can make all the difference in a child's life. His love and care can be the deciding factor in helping a young one become who he or she was created to be."[22]
--Ed McGlasson

"I am ascending to my Father and your Father, to my God and your God."
--John 20:17

My (Dino) father and I often went fishing together. Seldom do I fish without thinking of very intense memories of Dad. He and I had some great times together. I was once introduced by a student who said, "He has a very well developed sense of humor." That humor was developed while watching my father. He and I had a plethora of stories based on our fishing adventures.

Many years after the passing of my father into heaven, I was in the Everglades fishing with a professional fisherman who happened to be a member of my church. He was catching about five fish to my one. He then asked a silly question. "Do you want to catch more fish?" Laughing I responded in the affirmative. He proceeded to explain to me that the process I used in baiting my hook with a worm was wrong. He proceeded to show me the correct way. I couldn't believe my response. I explained to him that my way was far better. It was at that moment that I began to consider what my motive was for telling a professional that I knew better than him. Here is my friend who is a professional, and I am questioning his instruction of putting on a worm. Then it dawned on me, I put the bait on the hook the way my father taught me. It was as

[22] McGlasson, Ed Tandy. *The Difference a Father Makes: Calling out the Magnificent Destiny in Your Children*. Atlanta, GA, USA: Amphelon Pub., 2004. 13.

if I was defending his honor. I continued doing it Dad's way and caught far fewer fish. The influence of a father is powerful.

When Jesus was raised from the grave the first person He appeared to was Mary Magdalene. She is the second most frequently mentioned woman in the New Testament. Only the mother of our Lord, Mary, is mentioned more. After the death of Jesus she goes to the tomb, and finds that Jesus is no longer there. She is frantic fearing that the body of the Lord was stolen. While in the garden next to the empty tomb Jesus commences a conversation with her.

Mary's life was amazingly changed when she met Jesus. She often accompanied Jesus in the Galilee area and she, along with other women, provided resources for Jesus. She is named for the town she came from and a number of scholars sense that she was wealthy and perhaps a faithful supporter of Jesus and His ministry. One thing is for sure, she is heartsick because Jesus is missing.

Jesus speaks to her in the garden saying only a single word, her name: "*Mary*". She knew that voice. It was a voice she had treasured in so many instances, and now that same voice was speaking her name. "Rabboni" she replied.

She reaches for him and in a few words Jesus gives her instruction. His instructions are, "Go". Go and tell my brethren two important realizations. I go to my God and your God. Mary, you have a God. Mary, you have a Father.

Think of it. Mary and every child of God have a father.

The suffering on the cross that Jesus the Messiah just experienced was part of the Father's plan to provide salvation to all those who would come to Christ.

The Apostles creed states: "*He was crucified, died, and was buried*".[23] By the order of the Heavenly Father, Jesus Christ rose again. The Roman Statesman, Philosopher Cicero who served as Roman counsel in the year 63B.C. speaking on crucifixion said, "It was the most cruel and shameful of all punishments. Let it never come near the body of a Roman citizen."[24]

[23] "Apostle's Creed." Christian Reformed Church. February 12, 2019. Accessed April 06, 2019. https://www.crcna.org/welcome/beliefs/creeds/apostles-creed.

[24] Wiersebe, Warren W. *The Bible Expositionary Commentary.* Wheaton, IL: Victor Books, 1989. 382.

It was the Father who ordered this for His Son. Why did He do this? He did this in order that all the Mary's of the world might be in His family. It seems overwhelming that the Father would do this.

Stop and think about this Heavenly Father. He is a loving Heavenly Father. "*See what great love the Father has lavished on us, that we should be called children of God! And that is what we are*!" (1 John 3:1). God the creator of the universe calls us his children, an act of pure love.

He is also a compassionate Heavenly Father. "*The LORD is compassionate and gracious; slow to anger, abounding in love.*" (Ps. 103:8). The compassion of our father in heaven is astounding, far greater than anything we will ever experience with others.

He is a faithful God. "*They are new every morning; great is your faithfulness.*" (Lamentations 3:23). God is a faithful Father, imagine someone who makes a promise and never goes back on their word. Someone who is faithful in all circumstances, this is the father that we have.

Our Father is a good God. "*Give thanks to the LORD, for he is good. His love endures forever.*" (Psalm 136:1). Not only is God the father loving, compassionate, and faithful, but he is also good. God wants good things in our lives if we are willing to accept the goodness that He offers.

This Father is a shepherding Father. "*The LORD is my shepherd, I lack nothing. He makes me lie down in green pastures, he leads me beside quiet waters, he refreshes my soul. He guides me along the right paths for his name's sake.*" (Psalm 23:1-3). Shepherds were protectors of the flock. In the gospel of John, Jesus is described as a shepherd who is willing to lay down His life for His sheep (John 10:11)

He is a gracious God. "*The LORD is gracious and righteous; our God is full of compassion.*" (Psalm 116:5). Our Father is all of this and many of these attributes remind us of His paternal leadership in our lives. All of these are descriptions of God our Father. He is loving, compassionate, merciful, good, and gracious.

In this world we live in, sadly, not all fathers live up to this. There are some who are fatherless, and some fathers do not reflect these qualities, for those who had a father like mine consider it a blessing. For those who have fathers who do not live up to these qualities, know that there is a father in heaven who fulfills all of these qualities.

Although Jesus is the Son of God, He regularly reminded people about His Father. There has never been a closer relationship with the Father than what Jesus had. Jesus said, *"I and the father are one"* (John 10:30). Regardless of our personal relationship to our father we have a Father in heaven *"who has qualified you to share in the inheritance of the saints in the kingdom of light."* (Colossians 1:12). This Father gave the very best He had, He gave His Son to qualify us through His sacrifice to be members of His Kingdom.

I often think back on my father's influence in my life. He enjoyed a good joke. He loved being with family. He taught me much about life I miss him. The fact is I will see him again. However, I have a Heavenly Father that will never leave nor forsake me.

He is our Heavenly Father.

MIDRASH

"Jesus likely began his Bible study in a traditional way. The Bible he studied was the Old Testament. He did not just memorize or repeat its verses. The ways he studied it were shaped by the methods and tools of a group of Jewish teachers known as the Rabbis. The Rabbis puzzled over, debated, and cherished each word. They filled in gaps with magnificent stories that shed light on what God intended us to do or learn."[25]
--Evan Moffic

"You have heard that it was said to the people long ago… but I tell you."
--Matthew 5:21-22

SEVERAL YEARS AGO I (JONATHAN) ATTENDED AN ART EXHIBITION IN MIAMI Beach, Florida. Those in attendance had the opportunity to view works from new and upcoming artists, as well as some more well-known pieces, many of which were for sale. As I perused the art gallery I was struck by a small abstract painting about the size of a sheet of paper. The painting looked as though someone had taken a paintbrush and simply splattered paint all over the canvas. I spent a moment looking at the work trying to find the deep hidden meaning behind the splotches of paint, and after a few minutes I concluded that this work was simply an artist who had given up and thrown paint on the canvas. My brother Adam, who is a graphic artist and student of art with a much greater knowledge and appreciation of art, was with me. I asked him if he could see the deep meaning behind the seemingly random blotches of color and he was just as lost as I was.

The work made absolutely no sense to me. I was even more surprised

[25] Moffic, Evan. *What Every Christian Needs to Know about the Jewishness of Jesus: A New Way of Seeing the Most Influential Rabbi in History.* Nashville, TN: Abingdon Press, 2016. 94.

when I looked at the asking price: four million dollars. I couldn't imagine that anyone would pay such an exorbitant price for what looked like a four year old's art project. It was at that point that a couple walked up next to me admiring the work, I could tell that they were serious art enthusiasts, because they were accompanied by a man with an official looking badge on his shirt that identified him as someone who was a curator at the art show. I stayed close behind them because I wanted to listen in on their conversation to get their perspective on this baffling work. The couple listened as the man explained the deep meaning behind the splotches of paint on the small canvas, he explained that the colors were evocative of a certain period of this particular artists work. With great enthusiasm and expertise the curator explained the meaning of the work and how each color and each splotch was carefully constructed. The couple was sincerely interested in the painting and thought the four million dollar price tag worthy of consideration. At the end of the experts explanation I suddenly had a greater appreciation for this work of art, where I at one point saw random blotches, I now was able to perceive purpose and direction. All it took was for an expert teacher to give me the tools I needed to interpret the piece.

All art is subjective. The viewer is able to decide what value the art has, along with the meaning of the work. Viewing different works of art is a remarkable experience because each person has a unique response to each work. The beauty of art is that each individual person is able to interpret that art and decide what it means to them. When we read a passage of Scripture, is the experience any different?

Whenever we view a piece of art, read a story, or even listen to a text, we engage in the process of interpretation. If whatever we are engaged with is familiar to us, we most likely have in the back of our minds the correct interpretation of that work. We do this almost without thinking. For example, If I were to mention John 3:16, the familiarity of that passage immediately drives us to a particular understanding of what it means. We know already in the back of our minds the meaning of John 3:16, and we apply that meaning preemptively to the passage. We could refer to this as coming from our tradition. Our background and experiences can either clarify or distort the meaning of a text. Our experience with the passage informs what we think a particular text means.[26] Our understanding based on tradition is not necessarily a hindrance, but if that tradition locks us into a particular understanding without room for adjustment it limits our ability to see a variety of meanings in the text.[27]

As a first century Jew, Jesus would have been immersed in the text of the Scripture at a young age. The text of the Old Testament was the framing narrative for the people of Israel. As a young man, Jesus would sit at the feet of his elders and listen to the stories of his ancestors. He would learn the history of Israel from Abraham to Moses, to King David. Why was it so important for young men to learn these stories? In order for tradition and culture to live on, it must be passed down through the younger generations. This process for the ancient people of Israel would be known as discipleship. Discipleship was a unique relationship in which both the leader and the disciples had expectations. The disciples would follow their master, and in return they would be given access to the master's inner and outer life. "One story in the Talmud tells of a master who became disqualified when his inside did not match his outside."[28]

To illustrate just how important both the inner life and the outer life of the Rabbi was, the sages would often times rely on extreme examples. In the Talmud (a commentary on the Torah), we find the story of Rabbi Meir and his disciples. His disciples so wanted to be a part of every aspect of the Rabbi's life that one night when the Rabbi and his wife were in their bedroom about to be intimate with each other they heard a strange sound. Meir looked under his bed to find one of his disciples lying underneath. When asked what the disciple was doing

---

[26] Longman, Tremper. *Reading the Bible with Heart & Mind*. Colorado Springs, CO: NavPress, 1997, 52-59. Middleton, J. Richard & Walsh, Brian. *Truth is Stranger Than It Used to Be: Biblical Faith in a Postmodern Age*. Downers Grove, InterVarsity, 1995. Schultz, Richard L. *Out of Context: How to Avoid Misinterpreting the Bible*. Grand Rapids, MI: Baker Books, 2012. Raschke, Carl A. *The next Reformation: Why Evangelicals Must Embrace Postmodernity*. Grand Rapids, MI: Baker Academic, 2004. Chapter 5. Westphal, Merold. *Whose Community? Which Interpretation?: Philosophical Hermeneutics for the Church*. Grand Rapids, MI: Baker Academic, 2009, 71 ff.

[27] McKnight, Scot. *The Blue Parakeet: Rethinking How You Read the Bible*. Grand Rapids, MI: Zondervan, 2008.

[28] Moffic, 2016. 63.

there, he responded "this too, is Torah and I must understand it."[29] This exaggerated example that relies on humor is meant to show just how closely a disciple was meant to follow the master.

A clear example of this is the life of the apostle Paul. In Acts 22:3 Luke tells us that Paul studied under Gamaliel one of the most famous Rabbis in the first century (who was possibly the grandson of Hillel). The normal course for a young Jewish boy's life was this: at five the boy would learn to read the Scriptures, at ten he would begin to read the Mishnah (an ancient commentary written by the Rabbis on the Torah). At thirteen (Bar Mitzvah age) he would take on the full responsibility of a man to carry out the Laws of God found in the Torah. At eighteen he would be ready to be married.[30]

Paul learned from Gamaliel and became his disciple. As Paul learned and grew he would carry on Gamaliel's legacy by coming up with new interpretations of the Scriptures that would reflect the teachings of his Rabbi. So far we have seen that Jesus felt free to interpret the Scriptures in new ways, providing new meanings for his followers. The question remains how then do we read and interpret the Bible for ourselves; what criteria does Jesus set up?

A Rabbi was a professional scribe who would not just teach his students to memorize passages from the sacred text, but how to live them out as well. This process of taking a text, examining the text for meaning, and then interpreting and applying the text to modern day situations is known as a Rabbi's midrash. *Midrash* is a Hebrew word that means to search out.[31] To read the Bible in this way is to read a text, and then struggle with the text. The Rabbi would ask questions of the text, to seek out the missing pieces of a story. The Bible contains many stories with unanswered questions (one of the first examples of this is the origin of Cain's wife in Genesis 4:17). These puzzles are not meant to be explained away, but rather struggled over; this process of turning these questions over and over in our mind is a type of interactive and

---

[29] Ibid., 66.

[30] Achtemeier, Paul J., Joel B. Green, and Marianne Meye. Thompson. *Introducing the New Testament: Its Literature and Theology*. Grand Rapids, MI: Eerdmans, 2006. 289.

[31] Moffic, 2016.

dynamic reading.[32] In the Gospels Jesus asks 307 questions, and he only answers three of them. Jesus was a different type of Rabbi, because he taught with open ended questions.[33]

> "Midrash reads the Hebrew Bible not for what is familiar but for what is unfamiliar, not for what's clear but for what's unclear, and then wrestles with the text, passionately, playfully, and reverently. Midrash views the Bible as one side of a conversation, started by God, containing an implicit invitation, even command, to keep the conversation—argument, story, poem, prayer—going."[34]

Midrash sees reading a text as a conversation, one in which both sides are active. God has spoken to us in His word, but we must join the conversation as active partners questioning, probing, and searching out new meanings of a passage. We are not passively reading a passage for a simple objective meaning, rather we are actively engaged. Like turning a brilliant diamond to see each facet reflect the light, we turn the passage over in our minds to find its meaning.[35]

All Jewish males would long to study under the great Rabbis. When others referred to Jesus as Rabbi, what they were inferring was that Jesus was a teacher of the Scriptures whose job it was to pass along to others the multiple meanings of passages to disciples (John 3:2). Jesus as a Rabbi offered many different interpretations of Old Testament passages. "The Rabbis puzzled over, debated, and cherished each word. They filled in gaps with magnificent stories that sought to shed light on what God intended us to do and learn."[36] The Rabbis were storytellers who filled in the gaps of the Biblical text with parables and

---

[32] Enns, Peter. *Inspiration and Incarnation: Evangelicals and the Problem of the Old Testament.* Grand Rapids, MI: Baker Academic, 2005.

[33] Ibid., 69.

[34] Kunst, Judith M. *The Burning Word: A Christian Encounter with Jewish Midrash.* Brewster, MA: Paraclete Press, 2006, 4.

[35] Bell, Rob. *Velvet Elvis: Repainting the Christian Faith.* Grand Rapids, MI: Zondervan, 2005, 61.

[36] Moffic, 2016. 94.

lessons gleaned from their studies. In the gospels whenever Jesus tells his audience a parable, he is doing the job of a Rabbi. Each individual Rabbi would have his own unique interpretation of a passage referred to as his "*yoke*" (Matthew 11:29).[37]

This process involved a constant retelling and re-imagining of stories. Reading the Bible in this way takes the experience of the text from static to dynamic. Instead of retelling stories and applying the same meanings, teachers could now plumb the depths of the text to ask questions and fill in the gaps. As a teacher Jesus goes beyond traditional interpretations with his disciples.

In Matthew 8, a would be disciple is interested in following Jesus, but unfortunately his father has recently passed away, and the disciple asks Jesus for patience before he can fully commit to following Him. Jews in the first century believed that giving a proper burial for the dead was a divine directive (Genesis 23). In the ancient world burial was a two-step process. After death the body would be placed in a casket and buried in a tomb so that it could decompose. The family would then sit in Shiva (mourning) for seven days. The body would lie in the casket for approximately one year, during that time the body would decompose. After decomposition was complete the body would then be exhumed, and the bones would be collected and put in an ossuary. Those bones would then be reburied again for good. This entire process was known as the burial process, so when the man says that he must bury his father he was likely in the midst of this process.[38] Jesus response to the request would have been shocking for his audience *"Follow me and let the dead bury their own dead"* (Matthew 8:22). The response is shocking because Jesus calls for disobedience of a commandment directly from God because the urgency of discipleship supersedes the need to properly care for those who have passed on. To be a disciple of Jesus is to be willing to go beyond the Law. Jesus in this case is teaching his disciples by challenging both tradition and the Mosaic Law.[39]

In Mark 7 we find an example of a teaching that every Rabbi would pass on to their disciples. The teachers of the Law confront Jesus because

---

[37] Bell, 2005, 47.

[38] McKnight, Scot. *The Jesus Creed: Loving God, Loving Others*. Brewster, MA: Paraclete Press, 2004. 10-11.

[39] Sanders, Ed Parish. *Jesus and Judaism*. London: SCM Press, 2004. 252-255.

His disciples did not participate in the ceremonial hand washing before enjoying a meal together (John 2:6). Jesus rebukes the Pharisees and teachers of the Law for their lack of integrity because their uncleanness was a result not of what they did outwardly, but rather was the result of their inner lives being found lacking (Mark 7:15). In what would have been an astounding proclamation for all his hearers, Jesus then declares that not only do the disciples not have to participate in the ceremonial hand washing, but also in fact all foods are now clean (7:19). Jesus completely overturns the Jewish understanding of what food was kosher and what was not, and was therefore to be avoided. Even the disciples had a hard time with this teaching. They had been avoiding unclean foods their entire lives, and now all of a sudden they were to change their way of life? In Acts 10 Peter receives a vision from God in which he is again told that all foods are now clean. Despite hearing the teaching of Jesus previously, Peter still refused to eat unclean food out of a desire to be faithful to God. Peter needed a divine vision in order to change his mind. At this point in his life, even Peter could not faithfully live out the teaching of his master.

In the Sermon on the Mount Jesus repeats the phrase "*You have heard it said*" several times in his discourse (Matthew 5:21, 27, 31, 33, 38, 43). What Jesus is referencing here is the teachings of the different Rabbis. Jesus confronts the teachings of the Rabbis on a variety of issues including: murder, adultery, divorce, taking of oaths, and revenge. In each of these cases he begins with the traditional teaching on the subject, and then he applies a radical new understanding of what God's requirements are. Jesus quotes the Scripture, interprets, and probes behind the original Scripture to reveal new teachings.[40] What was the result of this radical teaching? "*...The crowds were amazed at his teaching, because he taught as one who had authority, and not as their teachers of the Law*" (Matthew 7:28-29). This new interpretation or *Midrash* on the Law was astounding because it was different from the teachings of other Rabbis. The teaching challenged his hearers to move in a new direction as disciples of Jesus.

One example of the differing interpretations of Scripture that Jesus would have challenged in the Sermon on the Mount (Matthew 5-7)

[40] McKnight, Scot. *Sermon on the Mount*. Grand Rapids, MI: Zondervan, 2013. 76.

is the Rabbinic teaching on divorce. Jesus is asked about divorce in Matthew 5:31-32. Different Rabbis addressed the issue of divorce and remarriage in the first century with different teachings all based on the same passage. Deuteronomy 24:1 says: *"If a man marries a woman who becomes displeasing to him because he finds something indecent about her."* Based on this single line, three of the dominant Rabbis of the day each had a different interpretation.

> The school of Shammai said: Let not a man divorce his wife unless he found in her some matter of indecency [immorality] as it is said, 'because he has found an indecency of something about her' (Deuteronomy 24:1). But the school of Hillel say: Even if she [merely] spoiled his food, as it says, 'because he has found an indecency of something about her' (Deut. 24:1). Rabbi Akiba says: Even if he found another woman prettier than her, as it says, 'and it turns out that she does not find favor in his eyes'" (Deut 24:1).[41]

Jesus offers his own interpretation as Rabbi in Matthew 5:32: *"But I tell you that anyone who divorces his wife, except for sexual immorality, makes her the victim of adultery, and anyone who marries a divorced woman commits adultery."* What Jesus wants to pass on to his disciples here is a radical new understanding of the importance of women. In the first century a woman was largely dependent on her husband for financial support. A divorced woman would have been looked down upon and labeled as undesirable. Jesus admonishes anyone that would follow him to take not only marriage, but the treatment of women with devout seriousness. To divorce a woman simply because she had burned dinner, and the subsequent disastrous consequences for the woman, was not the way that Jesus' disciples were to live their lives. As a Rabbi, Jesus was expected to have his own unique interpretations of Scripture and he would have regularly engaged in creative readings of the texts.

If Jesus freely re-interpreted Biblical passages through this creative

[41] Kugel, James L. *The Bible as It Was.* Cambridge: Belknap Press of Harvard University Press, 2000. 518.

reading that seeks to interact and play with the text (*Midrash*), how should we apply this to our world today? Does Jesus give us direction on how we should read and interpret Scripture? And more importantly, as a result of our readings, how should we behave if we want to truly be disciples that emulate our master? Shammai, Hillel, and Akiba all had different ways of interpreting a passage, and these differing interpretations split Jews into different groups. The followers of Shammai had a distinct way of acting in the world, as did the followers of Hillel, and Akiba. The teacher that you studied under formed your entire worldview.

The Jews in the first century were diverse; there was no univocal Judaism of the day because your master determined your perspective and your actions. Despite this, Jews were united at their core by one declaration, the *Shema*. The word *Shema* means "hear" and comes from a passage in Deuteronomy 6:4-5. *"Hear, O Israel: the Lord our God, the Lord is one. Love the Lord your God with all your heart and with all your soul and with all your strength."* This passage was to be prayed twice a day by faithful Jews and was the one aspect of religion that was common for all Hebrew people. No matter which Rabbi you studied under, you were expected to recite the *Shema* three times a day, morning, noon, and night.[42] It would have been repeated by Jesus daily starting early on in his life.

In Matthew we find Jesus repeating this passage when a teacher of the Law questioned Jesus about his personal interpretation of Scripture. It was common in the first century to ask a teacher what the most important commandments were. The Old Testament contains 613 commands, 248 of which are positive and 365 are negative.[43] It was necessary for a teacher to explain what the guiding principle of their teaching was. The most important Law for that particular Rabbi would inform all of their instruction, as it would be the lens through which they interpreted all Scripture. Jesus response is to quote the *Shema* as the most important commandment. *"Love the Lord your God with all your heart and with all your soul and with all your mind. This is the first and greatest commandment"*. It is at this point that Jesus adds to the quotation

---

[42] Moffic, 2016. 107-130.

[43] Wiersbe, Warren W. *The Bible Exposition Commentary*. Wheaton, IL: Victor Books, 1989. 81.

from Deuteronomy 6. He adds a quotation from Leviticus 19:18; *And the second is like it: Love your neighbor as yourself. All the Law and the Prophets hang on these two commandments"* (Matthew 22:37-40). Jesus takes the familiar prayer and adds to it. To add to something that was revered and repeated every day by the faithful would have been a radical new teaching for Jesus' disciples. In essence what Jesus says is that if you can master these two commands every aspect of your life will conform to my teaching and you will be a true disciple of mine.

The reason Jesus adds the second line about your neighbor is because this becomes the cruxt of how Jesus interprets all the Scriptures. Jesus tells his disciples that if our interpretation of a passage does not increase our love for God, then it should be re-evaluated. But, Jesus adds that all our interpretations should also lead to loving our neighbors. The question then becomes, how can we love our neighbor more, and of course, who is our neighbor?

The Pharisees were a group in the first century that took the question of who our neighbor was seriously. They intently studied the Torah as a way of life. They adhered to a strict interpretation of God's law, with the goal of creating a kingdom of priests within the Jewish people. This kingdom required a high degree of holiness. For the Pharisees, holiness meant ensuring that one observed the Laws of God carefully, and avoided those who did not. Their interpretation of the Law meant that fellowship should only be with others who were faithful in their observance of the Law, and this lead to a boycott of those who were non-observant of the Law. The most powerful example of this boycott can be found in their table fellowship, or who they would share a meal with. "To share a meal with a person was an expression of acceptance; to refuse to share a meal symbolized disapproval and rejection. Accordingly the Pharisees would not share a meal with the nonobservant."[44] The Pharisees interpreted the Scriptures according to holiness and separation, and that meant keeping anyone who was not like them at a distance.

This is why Jesus was often times criticized for eating with sinners (Mark 2:15; Luke 3:12, 5:29, 7:34, 14:1-6, 15:1, 19:1-10,).[45] The question

[44] Borg, Marcus J. *Jesus, a New Vision: Spirit, Culture, and the Life of Discipleship.* San Francisco: HarperCollins, 1991. 89.

[45] Achtemeier, Green, and Thompson. 2006. 167.

would have been asked: What kind of disciples are these? If a disciple was meant to emulate your life, tax collectors, sinners, alcoholics and sex-workers were not the type of disciples a Rabbi would welcome. When the Pharisees read the Old Testament they came to an interpretation that required them to separate themselves from these undesirables. Jesus read the Old Testament and came to a radically different interpretation. This interpretation was so radically different that he attached it to the most important prayer in the Jewish world. If one wants to study at the feet of Jesus and learn to interpret the Scriptures two important principles stand at the forefront, loving God and loving others. This is the lens through which all *Midrash* should be done.

If we want to be disciples of Jesus we should immerse ourselves in the Scriptures, and then live out the Scriptures in a manner that emulates our master. For the Pharisees, this meant creating isolated communities of holiness where the others were kept outside apart from them because they could in some way diminish their holiness. Jesus welcomes those very people, the outcast, the unworthy, the sinner. Not only does He welcome them, He eats with them. Eating with sent a powerful message to everyone in the community, that these were His neighbors, and as such we are called to love them in a greater way. Being a disciple of Jesus means that you no longer live your life in isolation from those who are considered unholy; rather you immerse yourself into a life that welcomes the outcast. This acceptance of others is truly what sets apart Jesus' disciples from others.

What is interesting about this teaching is the reaction that it causes amongst the other teachers of the Law. When other masters see the actions of Jesus they are appalled because of his acceptance of those who are unworthy. In Luke 15 Jesus tells three stories about three things that are lost; a sheep, a coin, and a son. In all three of these stories what was lost is found, the end result being a joyous celebration in heaven. Why does Jesus tell these three stories? Because Luke tells us that "*the Pharisees and the teachers of the law muttered, 'this man welcomes sinners and eats with them.'*" (15:2). What kind of discipleship is this? What kind of teaching is Jesus passing along to others that would allow them to be seen, even worse, to share a meal with these types of people?

The discipleship of Jesus is one of open arms and radical acceptance. Loving others means you can no longer keep them at a distance, we can no longer label them as outsiders or sinners; instead we must open our arms and welcome them. Christians have a long history of ignoring, castigating, and isolating those who are not like us. We distance ourselves from them based on labels: political affiliation, religion, gender, race, or orientation. Jesus comes to tell us there is a new way to interpret the Scripture and that new way means not excluding these people. That means welcoming them into our community, not as a threat to our holiness, but as full members, regardless of their current lifestyle. If you want to know if you are living as a disciple of Jesus, if those people in your life that you accept, love, and welcome are causing others to mutter behind your back you might just be on the right track. If others are surprised by the company you keep, you might be learning to interpret the Scriptures the way Rabbi Jesus would.

If your reading of the Scriptures makes your world smaller, and excludes more people, you are not reading the Scriptures in the way Jesus read them. When I was at the art museum I came across a painting that was worth millions of dollars, but all I could see were abstract blotches of paint. Because of my lack of knowledge, and not having a teacher to show me the true value of the piece, I missed out on the power and meaning of the work. When we read the Scriptures and use them to exclude others, we are not reading in the way of Jesus. All of our interpretations should lead us to love God and others more. Maybe instead of using our faith and interpretations to exclude more people a better way forward would be to do what Jesus did, and invite them into our community. This community would be wide and gracious and accept others. We would be less concerned about them tampering with our holiness and more concerned about welcoming them into our lives because that is the way Jesus would want his disciples to act. If we want to be disciples and study under Rabbi Jesus we must be willing to accept those who are considered outsiders and sinners.

The word *Midrash* might be a word that you have never heard before, but it is a powerful word that changes the way we read the Scriptures. And if we read the Scriptures in the same way that Jesus read and interpreted them we might even be accused of being gluttons and drunkards as a result, and we would be in great company (Luke 7:34).

EXCHANGE

"Gray hair is a crown of beauty when it is found in the way of righteousness."
--Solomon

"Unless your righteousness surpasses that of the Pharisees and the teachers of the law, you will certainly not enter the kingdom of heaven."
--Matthew 5:20

It was a hard day for me (Dino). I always admired Richard Nixon. When he ran for president in the 1960 election he was "my candidate". When he lost I remembered how I was so proud of him. The election was one of the closest in American history. John F. Kennedy won the popular vote by a slim margin of approximately 100,000 votes. Vice President Nixon won more states than his opponent but President Kennedy had more electoral votes. Kennedy had 303 electoral votes, slightly over the 270 to win. There are people today who still doubt the outcome. There were two states whose votes were razor thin. One was Illinois with Kennedy pulling out the victory by 9,000 votes and Texas with a differential of 46,000. With those two states Nixon would have scraped out a small win. At the time Nixon's home state of California had Kennedy in the lead, but a count of absentee ballots gave the Vice President the win several weeks later. Claims abounded about stuffing the ballot box in Illinois and Texas. Nixon's decision was to be admired. Journalist friend, Ed Mazo was prepared to write an article exposing fraud when Nixon told him to refrain. "Our country cannot afford the agony of a constitutional crisis"[46], was Nixon's response.

[46] "The Drama behind President Kennedy's 1960 Election Win." National Constitution Center-Constitutioncenter.org. Accessed April 07, 2019. https://constitutioncenter.org/blog/the-drama-behind-president-kennedys-1960-election-win/.

I so admired Mr. Nixon then. However, it is a fact of American history that the Watergate scandal saw a different side to him. In the second term of President Nixon, five men were found guilty for breaking into the Democratic National Committee headquarters prompting our president to plan a cover up and thus he lost his presidency. Nixon won in one of the greatest landslides in American history. In the 1972 election, Nixon won 520 electoral votes to 17 for George McGovern, the Democratic nominee with the Independent candidate John Schmitz receiving 0 electoral votes. Nixon was consumed with winning and destroying those who had given him such a difficult time. His view was to stop the leaking of classified information to the news media. In humiliation my president stepped down. The deep admiration I had for my president was not destroyed, but I did feel let down. In my judgment leadership took a hit in America and we are still reeling from it. Why? What was the purpose of brilliant men bungling such a ridiculous idea?

Since that day I have learned something about the human heart. None of us are righteous in and of ourselves. In what may be the greatest sermon ever delivered, Jesus spoke to His disciples on a mountain alongside the Sea of Galilee. The message is in Matthew chapters 5-7. Verses 1 -12 are the beatitudes. In verses 13-16 there is a command to be salt and light. Jesus explains how He fulfills the law in verses 17-20.

Matthew 5:20 has always energized my curiosity. When Jesus is explaining about the beatitudes I immediately feel quite guilty as I recognize I cannot possibly do what He is saying. I cannot in my own self do any of those things. Am I always meek? Do I always practice mercy? A few days ago a man who looked very destitute asked me for a ride in my automobile. My excuse, and believe me it is a good one, is that my wife was in the car with me and I must not put her at risk. Then I asked myself the obvious..."Would I do it if she weren't with me?" I'd rather not answer that, but I wasn't very merciful.

Do I always promote peace? These are only three of the beatitudes found in Matthew, and I struggle with all of them. Jesus then compares my righteousness with that of the scribes and Pharisees.

This is what Jesus said in Matthew 5:20. "*For I tell you that unless your righteousness surpasses that of the Pharisees and the teachers of the law, you will certainly not enter the kingdom of heaven.*" The question is: what was the righteousness of these religious leaders like? The scribes were the writers of the law. The Pharisees were known for giving to the poor, conducted lengthy public prayers, and they raved about their moral integrity. When Paul was a practicing Pharisee he claimed he was blameless. They performed these acts in the most public and conspicuous places. They had prayers suited to every occasion and were quick to correct other's inadequacies. They were passionate about recruiting zealots to follow their ways and promote their righteousness. Those who disagreed were in danger of punishment.

A good example is the Apostle Paul who set out to imprison members of the Way, the early followers of Christ. These religious leaders depended on their works for acceptance from God. The scribes were the doctors of law. They possessed the key of knowledge and interpretation. The Pharisees were separatists. Jesus is pointing out that they are righteous to many beholders. Yet Jesus, the Savior, who is so merciful and kind, reserved his most stunning denunciations of these religious leaders.

Notice the following passage of Scripture, "*While all the people were listening, Jesus said to his disciples, 'Beware of the teachers of the law. They like to walk around in flowing robes and love to be greeted with respect in the marketplaces and have the most important seats in the synagogues and the places of honor at banquets. They devour widows' houses and for a show make lengthy prayers. These men will be punished most severely.*'" (Luke 20:45-47). The issue with the scribes and Pharisees was that they were actors, hypocrites! They said one thing, pointed out the sin in others, lived a life of fraudulent activity in comparison to others. They added to sound teaching their own concepts. Jesus does not doubt their righteousness externally, but it is not an internal desire. Jesus in the beatitudes teaches something that is impossible to live up to, unless there is divine intervention. In a similar teaching to the disciples our Lord states, "*I am the vine; you are the branches. If you remain in me and I in you, you will bear much fruit; apart from me you can do nothing.*" (John 15:5). I can do nothing outside of Christ.

A term that we all need to become familiar with is the exchanged life. It refers to our identity in Christ. Missionary J. Hudson Taylor in his book, Spiritual Secret, coined the term The Exchanged Life.[47] The Christian partakes of eternal life at the moment they accept Jesus Christ as their Savior. The believer identifies with the crucifixion, burial, resurrection, and ascension of the Lord. The old person is to die daily while there is the exchange for the new man. This is only possible with Christ living His life through our lives. The fact is, we are all capable of the Watergate break in or a cocky arrogance and pride like the scribes and Pharisees, and what makes it worse is that when we are delivered of those sins we spend our times casting judgment on those who commit them.

Righteous is a word that can make us feel inferior, but when we are living the exchanged life, it is the faithfulness of God that makes us whole.

Righteousness is a powerful thought. My righteousness is nothing. Christ must live through me.

---

[47] Taylor, Howard, and Howard Taylor. *Hudson Taylors Spiritual Secret.* Chicago: Moody Press, 1993.

ROCK

"When Jesus first gave what we now call the Sermon on the Mount, he was staging something that would look to us much more like a political rally. He was like someone drumming up support for a new movement, a new great cause. He was calling his hearers, quite simply, to a new way of being Israel, a new way of being God's people for the world."[48]
--N.T. Wright

"The rain came down, the streams rose, and the winds blew and beat against that house, and it fell with a great crash."
--Matthew 7:27

I (JONATHAN) HAVE ALWAYS BEEN KNOWN AS AN INSTIGATOR.

Being the oldest of three boys in my family it comes to me almost as a birthright. Having two younger brothers meant that I was the one who normally instigated whatever trouble we were getting into as young boys.

One beautiful summer day when I was 5 years old, my mother heard a knock on the door. When she answered the door there was a stranger on our front porch with my brother, and I, cowering in shame behind him. The stranger was kind enough to inform my mother that we were standing at the end of the dirt road we grew up on throwing rocks at cars as they zoomed past us. Before a concerned motorist took the time to stop his car, inspect the damage that we had done with our projectiles, and load us into his car and take us back to our house at the end of the dirt road, we had caused quite a bit of damage. The total number of cars that we hit with rocks that day is still a mystery. What also has been unexplained is our motivation for throwing rocks in the first place. Since

[48] Wright, N.T. *The Original Jesus: the Life and Vision of a Revolutionary,* Grand Rapids, MI: W.B. Eerdmans, 1997. 48-49.

I was only 5 when I decided throwing rocks at cars was a good idea, I still cannot remember what inspired me to drag my brother to the end of our road.

Being the oldest brother meant that I deservedly took the brunt of the punishment for our misbehavior. Throwing rocks at cars must have seemed like a good idea at the time in my 5 year old brain, a perfect way to spend a summer day. Needless to say the punishment that came after we were caught convinced me otherwise.

A rock plays an important role in one of the first sermons that Jesus ever gave. In Matthew 5-7 Jesus gives an extended sermon. Matthew's gospel is organized around 5 major messages of Jesus, this being the first one recorded (Matthew 5-7; 10; 13; 18; 23-25). These 5 major sermons are meant to mirror the Pentateuch in the Old Testament. When readers of the Bible think of the Law, they normally think of the first five books of Moses (Genesis, Exodus, Leviticus, Numbers and Deuteronomy). These five books are called the Pentateuch, and Jews recognize it simply by the name Torah which means teaching or instruction[49]. Matthew structures his entire gospel around five major messages of Jesus which constitutes the new Torah or new Law for the people of Israel. Matthew wants his readers to recognize that these five sermons represent Jesus' basic teaching or instruction. They are the new Torah that his followers will live by.

Richard Rohr cites the Sermon on the Mount as being the closest record of the true teaching of Jesus that we find in the Scripture.[50] Scot McKnight has called the sermon the greatest moral document of all time.[51] If you were to read the gospel of Matthew from beginning to end, this would be the first sermon of Jesus that you would encounter. The reader should recognize this sermon as the starting point for everything Jesus is going to do. In the Old Testament, the first five books of the Bible are written in part to answer the question, what is God going to do to fix this? Immediately after the creation story the world goes astray, and the rest of the Torah seeks to provide guidance relating to how God will fix the mess that has arisen. In the New Testament, Jesus' followers are

---

[49] Schnittjer, Gary. *The Torah Story: An Apprenticeship on the Pentateuch.* Grand Rapids, MI: Zondervan, 2006.

[50] Rohr, Richard, and John Feister. *Jesus Plan for a New World: The Sermon on the Mount.* Cincinnati, OH: St. Anthony Messenger Press, 1996.

[51] McKnight, Scot. *Sermon on the Mount.* Grand Rapids, MI: Zondervan, 2013.

asking the same question. How can we fix the mess that we are in? Jesus offers a way to live a solid life built on a firm foundation in this sermon.

The sermon found in Matthew 5-7 is known as the Sermon on the Mount because Jesus ascends to the top of a mountain in Galilee to speak to the crowds that were following him. *"Now when he saw the crowds, he went up on a mountainside and sat down"* (Matthew 5:1). This is reminiscent of Moses who ascended a mountain to receive the Law (or instruction) from God in the Old Testament.[52] *"Then Moses went up to God, and the LORD called to him from the mountain"* (Exodus 19:3). He returns a short time later with direct instruction from God written on two stone tablets (Exodus 20). After ascending to the top of the mountain Jesus sat down, as was the custom of first century teachers before they would teach their followers (Mark 4:1; Luke 4:20, 5:3).

The sermon begins in a most unusual way with what is known as the beatitudes. In a series of short sayings, Jesus turns the social order of the day upside down. In this sermon it is the meek who inherit the earth, those who are in mourning are blessed, and those who are persecuted are to be considered to have an advantage (5:3-10). The implication of these words is that for Jesus' followers, the social order of the world, is being upended. No longer is it the strong who are on top, rather it is the weak. It is the meek, merciful, and the peacemakers who are the true leaders. These familiar sayings of Jesus are grounded in a political reality. The blessings in this passage are inextricably tied to the coming Kingdom of heaven. Anyone hearing these words would immediately understand the political undertones of the message.

> *"Anyone who was heard talking about the reign of Israel's god would be assumed to be referring to the fulfilment of Israel's long held hope. The covenant god would act to reconstitute his people, and end their exile, to forgive their sins. When that happened, Israel would no longer be dominated by the pagans. She would be free. The means of liberation were no doubt open to debate. The goal was not."*[53]

---

[52] Ibid. 2013.

[53] Wright, N.T. *Jesus and the Victory of God*. Minneapolis: Fortress Press, 1997. 151

What the audience in Jesus' day was looking for was a fresh work of God in the world. They were beaten and downtrodden, but one day that would all change because God would intervene in the world. The people listening to Jesus' sermon were anxiously anticipating a new reality, a new kingdom. When that kingdom began to break into the world they would be ready to act decisively. Their expectation was that one day they would rule with might and power, but Jesus' sermon seems to indicate the exact opposite. Instead of gaining more power, those who give up power and are humbled are those who are members in Jesus' kingdom.

When Jesus speaks about the kingdom of heaven, the underlying political message would be heard loud and clear. Those currently in power via political and military strength will not always have their place as rulers over us. A new kingdom was breaking in, and you could join the movement of God. Those who were faithful to God were patiently waiting for the right time to spring into action. Those in the audience for Jesus' sermon that day would have heard his message as a call to a new movement. If we understand the climate of the day Jesus' call to action will become all the more clear. Jesus was not the first teacher to call others to follow him during this time, but those movements looked far different than the one Jesus calls his disciples to. Instead of meekness, mercy, and peace, these movements offered a much different route.

During the time of Jesus the land of Israel was subject to several small scale revolts that had to be put down by the Roman Empire. The Roman Senator Tactius writes that during the reign of Tiberius (14-37 A.D.) there were no major wars in Palestine, which simply means the Roman Empire was able to put down all the rebellions without having to call up further troops from the North.[54] Revolts both on the large and small scale were common throughout this period.[55] Most uprisings were quickly put down by the Roman army in the area because of their superior military power. Despite these setbacks, the Jews of the day longed for the moment to come when they could finally overthrow their

---

[54] Wright, N. T. *The New Testament and the People of God*. Minneapolis, MN: Fortress Press, 1994.

[55] Crossan, John Dominic. *How to Read the Bible and Still Be a Christian: Struggling with Divine Violence from Genesis to Revelation*. New York: Harper One, 2016. 143-156.

oppressors. At several explosive moments in history, activists would leap into action, willing to give up their lives for the cause.

In the year 4 B.C. Herod the Great was overcome with illness; when word of Herod's illness spread, two young Jewish men decided that this was the time for symbolic action against the Roman Empire. Inspired by Judas and Matthias a group of freedom fighters embark on a daring and dangerous mission to cleanse the temple. It was common in the day for a symbol or idol to be put in a temple to represent the god worshipped there. Herod erected a giant gold eagle which was placed at the gate of the Jewish Temple in Jerusalem. The eagle was meant to be symbolic of the Roman Empire, much like a bald eagle would be symbolic for America. This was a way of honoring the Roman Empire, and for the Jews, this amounted to a blasphemous attack against their most holy place, and a clear violation of the first commandment (Exodus 20:3). Following Judas and Matthias' lead, this group of Jewish revolutionaries marched to the Temple Mount, and climbed to the top of the Temple gate. Using thick cords they lowered themselves down from the top of the gate and proceeded to cut down the eagle with axes.

Both Judas and Matthias knew that the penalty for this brazen act could be death, but for them this type of sacrifice was both necessary and justified. They were defending the cause of their god from the evil Roman Empire. Herod had dared to erect an idol in the most holy place, the Temple. Their zeal for God caused them to act in a brash and public way; they had hoped that their actions would cause a revolution amongst the people, the result of which would be a revolt against Rome and a new political reality in their homeland.

As this group of freedom fighters smashed the eagle with their axes, they found themselves surrounded by Roman soldiers. Their response to being caught sums up their fervor: "We shall die, not for any unrighteous actions, but for our love to religion."[56] These two men recognized their actions for what they were, a mix of political resistance to the empire, and a religious action. Judas and Matthias were able to lead forty Jewish men in their revolt, and all of them were arrested for their actions. These men believed radical action was necessary because

[56] Josephus, Flavius. *The New Complete Works of Josephus*. Grand Rapids, MI: Kregel, 1999. 17.159.

this was the moment when God would intervene. Their actions are defendable both in the political sense in that they were being oppressed by another foreign country, and in a religious sense because they were doing so out of zeal for the one true God.

A second example of the fervor of the people in the first century can be found in the book of Acts. In Acts 21 Luke recalls the story of Paul's visit to Jerusalem after his conversion. Paul travels to Jerusalem in order to meet with some leaders of the early church. While in Jerusalem Paul makes his way to the Temple area to participate in worship with his fellow leaders. Because Paul has been teaching that everyone (Jew and Gentile) can now be a part of the new people of God, the Jews rioted against Paul in the Temple area and accused him of bringing Greeks into the Temple (which would have been a violation of the rules of the Temple). The entire city is thrown into an uproar with Paul at the center trying to explain his purpose and clear his name.

The crowd dragged Paul from the Temple area and attempted to kill him on the spot. The local Roman authorities are informed of the chaos, and soldiers are dispatched to the Temple area. After the actions of Judas and Matthias, and later Jesus in the Temple (Matthew 21:12-13), Roman soldiers were always on call to deal with any unrest that might take place. The soldiers arrest Paul and immediately put him in chains. The mob was not satisfied with Paul simply being imprisoned, so they scratched and clawed their way forward to harm Paul. The mob is so unruly that the soldiers have to put Paul on their shoulders and carry him into the barracks so that he will not be killed by the angry crowd.

Once in the barracks the Roman commander wants to get the story straight. Outside he heard the shouts and cries of the mob, but he is still unsure of exactly who Paul is and what caused this uprising. The commander confuses him with another revolutionary character: *"'Aren't you the Egyptian who started a revolt and led four thousand terrorists out into the desert some time ago?'"* (Acts 21:38) Paul assures him that he is not "the Egyptian" and confirms his identity to the soldiers who have now taken him captive. Luke is silent about the identity of this Egyptian throughout the rest of his book, but obviously this person was someone who was on the radar of the Roman soldiers. So who exactly was this Egyptian, and what did he do to be placed on the Romans most wanted list?

The historian Josephus gives us the rest of the details about the

Egyptian.[57] The Egyptian was a prophet from Egypt who gathered unto himself several thousand followers. This prophet promised that the time had come for God to radically act in Israel, and that he was the prophet who God would use to bring about a new kingdom. The Egyptian recruited several thousand followers, and directed them to the Mount of Olives. The Mount of Olives is a small rise just outside the city of Jerusalem that overlooks the Temple. In the first century you could stand on the Mount of Olives and have a breathtaking panoramic view of the city of Jerusalem and the Temple.

The Egyptian promised his followers that God was going to radically act in history. He promised that the walls surrounding Jerusalem and the Temple would fall, reminiscent of the battle of Jericho in Joshua 6. The prophet would then lead his followers to military victory over the evil empire and restore the Temple to its former glory with the true people of God back in power. Unfortunately for the followers of this prophet, the walls did not fall. The Roman army was dispatched from the Temple area and 400 followers of the Egyptian are killed in a battle, with 200 captured and imprisoned. During the battle the Egyptian is able to slip away and escape, never to be heard from again. He remained a person of interest for the Roman army because of his ability to gain a following, and because of his violent aspirations of overthrowing the government.

These two episodes give us a feeling of the revolutionary fervor that existed in the time of Jesus. N.T. Wright sums up the feeling in and around Israel during this time:

> "Revolution of one sort or another was in the air, and often present on the ground, both in Galilee and (particularly) in Jerusalem, throughout the period of Roman rule. It was not confined to one group… whenever it was suppressed in one place it sprang up in another."[58]

At the center of both of these stories is the Temple, the most holy

---

[57] Ibid., 20.8.6.

[58] Wright, 1994. 176.

place in the land of Israel. The expectation of Judas, Matthias, and the Egyptian was that God would break into the present world and act in a decisive manner. A shift in the political world was coming, and the Temple was the center of all the attention. The Jewish hope for the renewal of their political fortunes, and the in breaking of the kingdom hinged on the rebuilding and cleansing of the Temple, while expectations of what the new political leader would look like varied in the first century, most agreed that cleansing and restoring the Temple would be a vital part of his ministry.

Why was the Temple the focus of all the revolutionary fervor?

For the nation of Israel the Temple of God is the location where heaven and earth are joined together. The Temple was the dwelling place of Israel's covenant God. The Temple was the operations center for all that God was doing in the world. If you wanted to be close to God while on earth, you would head to the Temple mount. In America if you want to see where the most powerful person in the country makes decisions you would make a trip to 1600 Pennsylvania Avenue. In Israel you would make your way to the heart of Jerusalem.

With this background in mind, imagine a scenario where a prophet and miracle worker is making his way through Galilee in the nation of Israel. With his inspirational teaching he has recruited many disciples. Some think he may just be the new spring of hope for a beleaguered people. As his following grows, he speaks of a new system, a new order, a new kingdom that will replace the current ruling elite.

This brings us back to Matthew 5-7 and Jesus' Sermon on the Mount. In several details Matthew calls our attention back to the nation of Israel as Jesus gives his sermon. He ascends a mountain like Moses did; this is the first of five sermons of Jesus in the book to echo the five books of the Law. Jesus begins His sermon by telling His audience that the kingdom would come, not through violence, military might, or revolution, but through meekness, peacemaking and persecution.

Judas, Matthias, and the Egyptian had come to lead the nation in revolt, but their revolutions failed, leading many astray. In Matthew 7:15-20 Jesus warns His audience that they should evaluate these other revolutionaries by the fruit that they produce. Those so called revolutionary leaders who took dramatic action against the evil empire of the day, only to fail to bring about a new world order should be evaluated by the type of people and the kingdom that they produce. As a tree is known by its fruit, you will be able to evaluate these other movements based on their actions.

Jesus' followers will be known by their fruit. The entire Sermon on the Mount is an explication of what the actions of Jesus followers will be. They will be a light in a dark world (5:14). They will not be prone to anger, and settle disputes in a fair manner (5:25). They treat women not as objects to be desired, but as full members of the people of God (5:27-28). They do not respond to violent actions against them with more violence because that simply keeps alive the vicious cycle. Rather they respond to those who persecute them with love and kindness (5:38-48). They are not out for the praise of others, but through prayer their lives are examples to others (6:1-18). Rather than looking down on others who are not like them, they have their arms open wide to everyone regardless of their faults (7:1-6). This is the fruit they produce that will separate them from all the other movements of the day (7:21-23).

Jesus closes the sermon with an illustration involving a wise and foolish builder. Often times when we hear these words we assume that Jesus might have been making a point about how to properly construct a home. He was after all a carpenter's son, and knew full well the importance of good craftsmanship. However, this is not a precursor to HGTV television programming. If we know the context of the day, the conclusion of this powerful sermon means so much more.

Jesus proclaims to his hearers that "'*everyone who hears these words of mine and puts them into practice is like a wise man who built his house on the rock.*'" (Matthew 7:24) The question is, what is the rock in this passage a reference to?

If you were to take a trip to Jerusalem today you would certainly want to visit the Temple mount. The Temple is no longer visible there, as it was destroyed by the Romans during yet another revolt by the Jews during the Jewish War of 66-73 AD. However, what you would find on the Temple mount is a Muslim mosque. This mosque was originally completed in the year 691 A.D. and remains one of the oldest examples of Muslim architecture in the world. The mosque is considered to be one of the most holy places for the one billion Muslims in the world. During the crusades of the 12th century the Crusaders conquered the city of Jerusalem and turned the mosque into a functioning church. Within a short period of time the mosque was recaptured by the Muslim leader Saladin and reinstated as a Muslim place of worship. Today it is an active Muslim mosque open for prayer and to curious visitors.

What is the name of this famous mosque? The Dome of the Rock.

It is named the Dome of the Rock because if you enter the octagon shaped mosque you will come face to face with a giant piece of stone jutting up from the center of the building. This gigantic rock emerges from the floor of the Dome of the Rock and sits just above the floor of the mosque. It is the centerpiece of the mosque. The dome is built around the rock, because of the importance of this stone in both Christian and Jewish history.

This stone is said to be the place where Abraham was going to sacrifice his son Isaac, the stone later became the foundation stone for what was the Temple in the time of Jesus. In Jesus day, the house built on the rock was a clear reference to the Temple. Just as the Temple was built on the rock, so Jesus says his followers can be like the man who builds his house on the rock (Matthew 7:24). The followers of Jesus will be the new Temple, one not of brick and mortar, but one of flesh and blood.

The conclusion of Jesus Sermon on the Mount is to call his followers to be people of the Rock, to be a community centered on the Temple. Such a person is always stable in all that they do because they have a firm foundation (7:25). When storms strike those who have built their foundation on the rock are able to withstand the wind and the rain because of their strong foundation.

When we think of a temple today, we often times think of a sacred place. A temple, church, synagogue or mosque is a holy place where we think we can encounter the divine. In the ancient world temples were constructed to be dwelling places for the gods. Because the people on earth needed a connection point to their gods, structures were built for them. The construction of these temples was done with the utmost care, because the gods the people worshipped would one day make their dwelling places in these earthly homes. This is the reason for the very specific instructions for construction of both the Tabernacle and the Temple in the Old Testament (2 Chronicles 2-5). Once the Temple was completed the work was finished off by the placing an image of the god in the Temple. Not because that image was the god, or had the power of the god, but rather because the image was a representation of the god.

When Jesus concludes His sermon with talk of a people built on the rock, He is saying that if we will follow His message we can be the new Temple people. We can be the ones who reflect God into the world by the way we treat others, the way we pray and fast in times of need and the way we break down barriers instead of excluding others (Matthew 5-7). God may not be visibly present, but He has placed His image in the world to act as a light to the world (Matthew 5:14). And what is that image? The image is human beings created by God to reflect His work in the world (Genesis 1:27).

A strong foundation is important not only for our homes, but for our lives as well. In this sermon Jesus calls us to be people of the rock, but that solid foundation does not come in the form of money, power, or fame. Instead Jesus tells us that those who are the most stable are those who serve others, are oppressed at times, and are willing to look beyond others faults to accept them unconditionally.

The word rock brings to mind stability and strength, if we are willing to take some of these counter-cultural steps we too can be people of the rock.

SPIT

"Two words one could never think of applying to the Jesus of the Gospels: Boring and predictable."
--Philip Yancey[59]

"He has done everything well... He even makes the deaf hear and the mute speak."
--Mark 7:37

It happened during a Monday Night Football game on December 15, 1997.

Over twenty years since it happened, I (Jonathan) can still remember the play because it involved one of the meanest players in the league performing an act that everyone found to be despicable.

Bill Romanowski played in the National Football League for sixteen years for four different teams. He was considered by many fans to be one of the toughest, nastiest players in the NFL during that time. Romanowski was a linebacker, which meant that his job was to tackle the player on the opposing team who had the ball, and Romanowski made a living inflicting as much pain as possible on his opponents. At the end of his career he was ranked the fifth dirtiest player in team sport history by ESPN.[60] Romanowski always played at the very edge of the rules, always looking for an advantage over his opponents. If this meant bending the rules or engaging in something others would consider unsportsmanlike, that was fine with him. This made him one of the most hated players in the NFL.

The victim in this case of unsportsmanlike conduct was J.J. Stokes.

---

[59] Yancey, Philip. *The Jesus I Never Knew.* Grand Rapids, MI: Zondervan, 1999. 23.

[60] ESPN. Accessed March 30, 2018. http://www.espn.com/page2/s/list/dirtiest/players.html

Stokes played in the NFL for nine seasons for three different teams. Stokes was considered an average Wide Receiver amassing over 4,000 receiving yards and 30 total touchdowns.

After an offensive play by the 49ers, as J.J. Stokes and Romanowski made their way back to their respective huddles, the two players began to argue over the previous play and some of the dirty moves used by Romanowski during the game. The Monday Night Football cameras caught them face to face arguing, and just before Stokes turned to head back to his teams huddle, Romanowski spit into the face of J.J. Stokes. I can vividly remember the moment I saw it happen, and was shocked. Arguments are common in team sports between players and at times pushing and shoving can occur (usually incurring a penalty). But to spit into someone's face is the ultimate example of disrespect. Romanowski was later fined $75,000 for the offense, and was widely criticized by the media and fellow players for his actions.

Spitting in someone's face is considered one of most disgusting actions you can make towards another person. I will never forget that Monday Night in December of 1997 because the play involved one player spitting into the face of another person. Spitting on someone is considered to be an incredible act of disrespect, and thereby memorable.

In Mark 7-8 we find two very peculiar and memorable miracles of Jesus. They are memorable for a few reasons, but one of the primary reasons they are hard to forget is because they involve spit.

> *"After he took him aside, away from the crowd, Jesus put his fingers into the man's ears. Then he spit and touched the man's tongue"* (Mark 7:33).

> *"He took the blind man by the hand and led him outside the village. When he had spit on the man's eyes and put his hands on him, Jesus asked, 'Do you see anything?'"* (Mark 8:23).

Why, in two successive chapters would Mark tell us that Jesus needed to spit on someone in order to heal them? In the first miracle in Mark 7, Jesus is able heal a deaf and mute man by spitting and touching the man's tongue. By spitting, Jesus is able to immediately heal the man.

Later in Mark 8, Jesus is brought a blind man seeking healing. However, in this healing a two-step process is required because after first spitting on the man's eyes he still is not entirely healed. The spit seems to cloud the man's vision even more, not allowing him to see clearly.

Why would Mark make note that Jesus spit on two people, and why would Jesus not be able to heal someone on the first try?

The first question we need to answer is the reason for the spit in both of these stories. First and foremost, the action of spitting on someone is extremely memorable. If you have ever had the misfortune of experiencing this, it is not an event that you are likely to forget. Spitting on someone is seen as so distasteful that it is burned into our memory forever. Imagine the reaction of the crowd, who brought the two disabled men to Jesus expecting healing. They were brought to this miracle worker in order to be made whole; they certainly did not expect Jesus to resort to spitting. If you were in the crowd would you have stepped up and protested? Would a fight have broken out because of the disrespect shown to the person in need?

Why does Jesus spit on the two men? Why would Mark, as he is writing his Gospel, include gross, very human action in these stories? When we think of Jesus, do we picture him spitting?

Part of the answer to those questions is the way human beings understand the divine. Throughout human history civilizations have tended to attribute to their gods human characteristics, because humans expected that the gods would react to situations in much the same way that a human being would. The gods are like us because we understand the world in terms of our own experience. The Greek pantheon is a great example of this, where gods were expected to act in jealousy, anger, and frustration much like human beings would.[61] The human experience was the point of reference, and that point of reference was applied to the gods. In Egypt the gods were depicted in multifarious ways. Sometimes the human depiction of a god was given the wings of an eagle or the head of a lion. The result of these additions was to make the god more memorable. A statue of a human being depicted as a god could simply be forgotten because of the ordinary nature of the idol, but a god depicted

---

[61] Cunningham, Lawrence S., and John J. Reich. *Culture & Values: A Survey of the Humanities.* 7th ed. Vol 1. Boston, MA: Wadsworth, 2010.

as a half man half lion would certainly be more memorable because of the conjoining of the two images.[62] These are examples of including radical or strange aspects to a god or story to make it more memorable. In the healing stories of Mark 7 and 8 Jesus spitting on those in need of healing make the entire story more memorable.

Another point needs to be made about the nature of miracles in the book of Mark. In both of these healing stories, the miracle itself is not meant to be a "proof" of the divine nature of Jesus. For Mark Jesus is the Son of God, the promised Messiah (1:1). However, these miracles are not necessarily meant to be proof of that divinity. In the ancient world healing was not necessarily a sign that the healer was a divine figure.[63] In the Exodus story Moses goes before Pharaoh, who immediately demands a sign from Moses' God. Aaron throws his staff down before the Pharaoh and it becomes a snake. Interestingly the Egyptian wise men, sorcerers, and magicians are able to perform the same miracle with their secret arts (Exodus 7:11-12). Jesus' disciples are also able to perform miracles (Mark 6:12; Acts 3:7-8). In the Scriptures these individuals are not considered divine; rather these miracles are an example of the power of God at work in the world. In the book of Mark miracles are not necessarily "proofs" of divinity. During the trial and crucifixion of Jesus, Herod was pleased to see Jesus because he wanted him to perform one of the miracles that he had heard so much about. Miracle workers were common throughout both the Old and New Testaments. In the gospels the miracles of Jesus are advanced signposts of what is to come in the new kingdom that Jesus is establishing. They are what C.S. Lewis would call glimpses of what is to come.[64] The ability to perform a miracle does not necessarily mean that you are a divine figure, rather it is evidence that God is working through you, empowering you for a particular purpose.[65]

Mark includes Jesus spitting in both of these miracles to make them more memorable, and as an advanced signpost of what is to come.

---

[62] Aslan, Reza. *GOD: A Human History.* S.I.: CORGI, 2018.

[63] Kirk, J.R. Daniel. *A Man Attested by God: The Human Jesus of the Synoptic Gospels.* Grand Rapids, MI: Eerdmans Publishing, 2016. (For a full scholarly defense of idealized human beings taking this role).

[64] Lewis, C.S. *The Great Divorce.* London: Collins, 2012.

[65] Kirk, 2016.

Immediately following these two stories, Jesus speaks of his impending death and the kingdom that will be established as a result (Mark 8:31 – 9:1). The disciples would not have expected or accepted that their leader would be killed. What type of Messiah would be put to death? Certainly not one who was truly powerful.

The second interesting aspect to this miracle is the requirement of a two-step process for the miracle to be fully effectual. After Jesus spits on the man's eyes he asks him: *"Do you see anything?"* (8:23) The man's response reveals that the healing is only partial. *"I see people; they look like trees walking around"* (8:24). Jesus then places his hands on the man's eyes a second time and his sight is fully restored so that he can see everything clearly. Why would Jesus need a second try to heal the man completely?

All of the gospel writers carefully select their material from a vast storehouse of anecdotes, sermons, and healings of Jesus that they were either witnesses to, or carefully researched (Luke 1:1-4; John 20:30). Each gospel is unique, and each author carefully arranges their material for their special purpose.[66] A clear example of this is the cleansing of the temple. For Matthew, Mark, and Luke the cleansing takes place near the end of Jesus' life (Matthew 21; Mark 11; Luke 19) and is one of the events that leads to his crucifixion. In the book of John the cleansing takes place at the very beginning of Jesus ministry immediately after His first miracle (John 2). The placement of the event is arranged according to the purposes the author has in mind. The same is true of the dual healing event in Mark 8.

In these two chapters Mark develops a theme of blindness, and failure to see the true vocation of the Messiah amongst the disciples. In Mark 8:1-21 we have the miracle of the feeding of the four thousand. A large crowd was following Jesus for several days with no food. This is the second feeding miracle in the book of Mark, both being quite similar. Why would Mark include two feeding miracles in his short narrative?

> *"Mark 8:14-21 makes it evident that Mark saw both feeding miracles as important revelations of Jesus'*

[66] Witherington, Ben. *Reading and Understanding the Bible.* Oxford: Oxford University Press USA, 2015. 88.

> *significance. His devoting space to two accounts of the same sort of miracle suggests that each one had for him a special significance and that neither could be omitted without losing something important."*[67]

Mark includes two separate and very similar feeding miracles to emphasize the inability of the disciples to truly understand the ministry of Jesus. Despite witnessing a very similar miracle earlier, the disciples are still blind to what is happening right in front of them.

Mark tells us that Jesus had compassion on the crowd and wanted to provide a meal for them. The disciples are confounded by this idea because they are in a remote place with no food available (6:36; 8:4). At the very first mention of trying to feed such a large crowd, the disciples are blind to the power of Jesus. Jesus proceeds to ask the crowd to sit down, and then with only seven small loaves of bread and a few small fish, Jesus is able to feed the entire crowd. Despite the disciples lack of faith the miracle was possible (8:8).

Immediately after the miraculous feeding the Pharisees ask Jesus for a miraculous sign (8:11). The Pharisees to this point were blind to the work of Jesus. Despite his previous feeding miracle, the Pharisees still cannot see Jesus as the true Messiah, the Son of God. Jesus is dismayed with their lack of faith and request for a sign because their request came from a place of spiritual blindness and lack of faith.

In Mark 8:14 we are informed that "*the disciples had forgotten to bring bread, except for one loaf they had with them in the boat*". Despite the abundance of bread just created by Jesus for the feeding of over 4,000 men the disciples have come away unprepared for the journey ahead of them. Jesus responds to them "*...Be careful... Watch out for the yeast of the Pharisees and that of Herod*" (8:15). The yeast that Jesus speaks of here is not literal yeast, but rather a warning of the false teaching of the Pharisees (Matthew 16:12). In their unseeing state, the disciples confuse Jesus' reference. They are sure they have no yeast with them, because of their lack of bread (8:16). Jesus is confounded at their myopic view of his ministry. In one of the most damning statements about the disciples in Mark he asks them "*Do you still not see or understand? Are*

[67] Hurtado, Larry W. *Mark*. Peabody, MA: Hendrickson Publishers, 2008.

your hearts hardened?" (8:17). This response from Jesus is an allusion to Jeremiah 5:21 and an echo of Isaiah 6:9-10. Both passages are in reference to the blindness of the nation of Israel in the Old Testament. This would be a stinging rebuke to the disciples who should by now understand Jesus' message. They had the great privilege of being eye witnesses to His miraculous works and His teaching, and yet they were still spiritually blind.

What exactly were the disciples unable to see? Mark 8 is a turning point in the gospel; it acts as a sort of fulcrum for the rest of the book. Immediately following this story Jesus sets His sights on Jerusalem, and eventually His impending death on the cross (8:31; 9:31-32; 10:32-34). Repeatedly Jesus clearly tells His disciples where things are heading. The Son of Man will be betrayed and handed over to His enemies who will eventually execute Him. And what was the response of the disciples to each of these revelations? The disciples were blind and had a complete lack of understanding (9:32)[68]. Surely Jesus would not die before he won victory over his enemies.

Time and time again Mark carefully lays out story after story of the disciples continued blindness, which leads up to the two staged healing of the blind man in Mark 8:23-26. The disciples were spiritually blind, and this man was physically blind. Both were in need of healing. As Jesus performed miracle after miracle the disciples remained blind. Jesus fed five thousand and the disciples did not understand. Jesus feeds another crowd of four thousand men, and the disciples are still unable to see the true vocation of the Messiah. The blindness of the disciples is mirrored in the man from Bethsaida (Mark 8).

Why then the two-stage healing of the blind man? Mark carefully constructs this healing to be both memorable (spit) and as an insight into how Jesus will deal with his followers. The miracle is not meant to prove that Jesus will reign supreme as a deity who can perform the miraculous. Instead, Jesus immediately signals that his ministry will end in the greatest defeat possible, death.

Sometimes it takes more than one miracle for them to understand the teaching of Jesus, and Jesus will be patient with His followers, because what He is looking for is progress. A step in the right direction

---

[68] Kirk,. 475.

is progress, one step closer to understanding the truth. And even though the disciples continually misinterpret the message of Jesus and his vocation, he continually reminds them of his true purpose. Like a patient teacher who works with a struggling student drilling information over and over in new ways, Jesus patiently and purposefully works with his disciples to get them to see the way.

For those of us today trying to understand the teachings, ministry, and way of Jesus in modern times, the road can be fraught with pitfalls and backsliding. We take one step forward in our spiritual journey, only to soon realize that shortly after we have fallen back two steps. If you are a member of a religious community of any sort you know the feeling of always falling just short of the expectations of others.

What this story shows us is that Jesus is not looking for perfection, but progress. Any step in the right direction is a positive one. Wherever you are on your faith journey, what Jesus is looking for is another step forward regardless of how small that step might be. Mark reminds us that the disciples saw not one, but two different feeding miracles of Jesus, and after each miracle they were blind to the message of Jesus. The same could be said of many of us in our faith journey.

Jesus uses a two-part miracle to show that sometimes the work of God is progressive. Think about your own faith journey, has it been one of steady progression? Or one of ups and downs, where there are times the down period is longer and more significant than those where you are making progress?

This is exactly what the disciples experienced. Despite being witnesses to Jesus' miracles and despite being able to listen to His teachings firsthand, they were still blind to what was going on. Jesus, like a good teacher remains patient, continually going over the lesson again and again until the disciples are able to take the next step forward. The faith journey is one of progress, not perfection. What Jesus is looking for is another step forward.

In our faith communities today we often times call others to make decisions of faith immediately, and expect a radical life change because of a single event or moment in time, but faith is a journey. Some individuals come to the Jesus story with baggage and doubts. Some reject the entire idea that anyone could go from blind to seeing because in our modern world we know that that sort of thing simply does not happen. For some the simple mention of religion, the church, or even the Bible causes them to shut down. Some further along in their faith journey have come to the point where they have questions, and some have completely given up on the faith they once had because it no longer seems sustainable.

For the faithful, faithless, doubters and skeptics Jesus is ready. The disciples who were eyewitnesses to Jesus work were blind just like we are. Jesus does not give up on them; instead he continually invites them to take one more step. In Mark 8 the healing of the blind man is a two-step process, not because Jesus could not heal the man with a single word, but because healing and growth is progressive.

Jesus is calling everyone to take the next step forward to continue on in their journey. Healing and faith in this passage are not instantaneous, they are a process. Wherever you are in the process of faith, Jesus invites you to continue, to take the next step forward.

Spit is gross, and memorable. Would you associate the word spit with Jesus? For Mark, spit is a unique way of showing us how Jesus works in stages, meeting us where we are at.

Spit is also Mark's way of inviting us into a journey, all we have to do is take the first step.

WATER

"Your work matters a great deal to God, to others, and to our world. There is no ordinary work. The work God has called you to do is extraordinary."[69]
--Tom Nelson

"Anyone who welcomes you welcomes me, and anyone who welcomes me welcomes the one who sent me."
--Matthew 10:40

I (DINO) APPROACHED THE PLATFORM OF THE CHURCH I WOULD BE SPEAKING at on a Sunday morning. I walked by the pulpit prior to the beginning of the service and noticed a middle-aged woman holding a glass of water. She looked at me and it was obvious that this water was meant for me. As I thanked her she startled me with the question, "How do you like your water?" My mind was preoccupied with the message that I would give and the expression on my face showed her that I was not ready to answer the question. Quite frankly I had never been asked that before. My first thought was to respond to her by saying with tongue in cheek "wet." It was obvious from her sincerity that this was not a joking matter. She helped me out of my embarrassing dilemma by introducing herself and then added: "This is something I do for speakers. It is a blessing for me to give you this water. Do you like it cold, hot, or lukewarm?" Not knowing how I wanted it my response was cold. "Good," she responded. "This one is cold." I set it on the pulpit. I normally do not sip water during messages, but I made sure I did this time.

Water is a tasteless, transparent liquid. Water flows. A warm shower is refreshing because of the water. Medical experts often remind us to drink eight glasses a day. If water drips on wood long enough it ruins the

[69] Nelson, Tom. *Work Matters: Connecting Sunday Worship with Monday Work.* Wheaton, IL: Crossway, 2011. 97.

timber. Weeping involves water. Grieving with tears helps us to grow emotionally. Tears help to relieve pain. Emotional tears release oxytocin and endorphins, thus allowing easing of emotional pain. Flowers, bushes, trees, plants, and fruit all grow with both water and sunlight. Water on a hot muggy day soothes a thirsty throat. Water can cause damage. Consider what a flood can do. Despite the fact that our home sits on a hill, we experienced the water damage of a flooded basement during a flood in 2011 where we live in upstate New York. Although we were able to repair our basement adequately, water can ruin a home. Stagnant water can produce disease and death.

I lived in Florida for fifteen years and would occasionally go to the beach. I found myself staring for a long time at something that was overwhelming. It was the ocean, full of water. Oceans, with their body of saline water compose a large part of the earth's hydrosphere. Salt water covers nearly three fourths of the surface of the universe. It is truly overwhelming. It is so much bigger than I can comprehend.

Jesus often used water as a metaphor. One such incident was a teaching He gave in Matthew 10: "*And if anyone gives even a cup of cold water to one of these little ones who is my disciple, truly I tell you, that person will certainly not lose their reward* (10:42). In the previous verses the Lord is using parallel concepts about receiving others. In verse 40 the emphasis is on Jesus. If someone receives Jesus he is also receiving the Father. In verse 41 the thought is receiving a prophet. Jesus uses a little thing, he calls it a cup of water. He calls it a cold cup. It seems insignificant, but it can make a difference. A cup of cold water is a blessing when you are thirsty. In the ancient world a drinking cup could be anything. Water was in short supply. There are three very helpful usages here to understand the Master's teaching.

First, in the ancient days in the hot climate, wells were the place to get refreshment. Jesus' famous conversation with the Samaritan woman was at a well (John 4). She is commonly referred to as "the woman at the well." This place appears to be a meeting place where courtesies and conversation were common. It is here where people could get caught up on the news from the villages. Drawing water was the goal, but the fellowship was similar to Americans going to a coffee shop to get coffee with a deeper purpose to enjoy fellowship, organize a meeting, or plan an event.

Jesus in Matthew 10 is giving some practical advice concerning the kind of reception the disciples would have in their travels. In the beginning of the chapter Jesus sends them to the "*lost sheep of the house of Israel*" (10:6). The lost sheep are the Jews who have not yet recognized their Messiah was with them. At this time they were not to go to the Samaritans or Gentiles. They are being sent on a preaching mission. As noted in verse 41, preachers should be treated with the greatest respect because of the Savior they represent and proclaim. Throughout scripture there are many Christian leaders who were disrespected. Those who were the culprits had to deal with the results. Examples are the Moabites and their treatment of Gideon (Judges 6-9) and Herod's demise after his dealing with the Apostle Peter (Acts 12). We are taught in Matthew 10 that the prophet is to be treated with respect and kindness. This leads to our third usage.

There seems to be a progression in the chapter. There is a descending in the order of the words Jesus gives. The beginning of the chapter is a reference to the Father and then there is the Son, prophet, a righteous man, and a little one. Jesus came to die for the world in order that there might be salvation to all who believe. The little one here seems to be a reference to the servant. The cup of cold water is given in the name of a disciple. We as disciples are here to serve. In God's kingdom it is not the "big shots," but the servants who are recognized for their place in the Kingdom and through acts of service and courtesies to others are giving blessing and glory to God! A cup of water may seem like an insignificant gift; however, if it is given in the name of the disciple who is proclaiming Christ, it has its reward! In the hot climate of the Judean region, people had to use a water well to obtain clear, fresh water. Giving a cup of cold water was a very common thing to do. It is a small act of benevolence and charity that was commonly practiced at the time.

The book of Judges adds an interesting thought to this discussion. "*You who ride on white donkeys, sitting on your saddle blankets, and you who walk along the road, consider the voice of the singers at the watering places. They recite the victories of the LORD, the victories of his villagers in Israel. "Then the people of the LORD went down to the city gates*" (Judges 5:10-11). Note the watering places were the location for refreshment, fellowship, and worship. The blessings are extended to those we serve and the satisfaction is for the one who gives the cup of water. The cup of water may be a gift of money, an act of kindness of cleaning an invalid's house, giving a ride to the doctors for someone not able to drive, or any number of other acts of kindness that may seem insignificant, yet the cup is huge for the respondent.

Additionally, this is a good day to think of one of God's servants. Maybe it is your pastor or your life group teacher. Maybe it is a person who has meant much to you. Perhaps it is someone who is alone or in need of an encouraging text, email, or cell phone call. Send them a cup of cold water. Maybe it is a thank you note. Perhaps it is a gift certificate to their favorite restaurant. Your cup is an encouragement to you and them.

I became a pastor in 1970. Over a three year period our church grew beyond my wildest imagination. Our church moved to a new location on what is today over 50 acres of property. When our church relocated to our new campus our church auditorium seated over 1,200 people. It was full every Sunday morning and I was under 30 years of age. The thought of preaching to all those people was very exciting, and yet fearful. I worked intensely to prepare and deliver the messages. I often wondered if I was connecting with the congregation. After the Sunday morning service my wife and I would go to the back of the church auditorium to shake hands, greet people, and listen to prayer concerns. As the crowd slowly left the church I would walk to my office and relax for a few moments in my easy chair. Sunday after Sunday I would notice a small piece of paper under my door. I would pick it up and read a hand written note. It was always the same hand writing. The note contained encouragement for me. The information was up to date and made mention of the sermon topic I had just delivered. The words were uplifting and very encouraging. Those words were such a blessing to this young pastor. They were literally a symbolic cup of cold water. Week after week the notes were there. One week I went around the corner early after a Sunday morning to see if I could find who was slipping the notes under the door. No one came by. I went to my office and to my surprise there was the note. Eventually I found out who was doing this. A young, godly woman in our church dropped those notes under my office door. Upon learning that I knew, her response was something like: "I wanted to be an encouragement to our new pastor." Believe me that was a cup of cold water.

Water, it is essential for life. A glass of cold water is any deed done in service to others. The next time you see the word "water", remind yourself that every good work that you do does not go unnoticed. In 1 Corinthians 15 Paul concludes his marvelous chapter on the resurrection with these words: "*...always give yourselves fully to the work of the Lord, because you know that your labor in the Lord is not in vain.*" No matter how big or how small your cup of water is, it matters to God.

LIGHT

"Jesus came to dispel the darkness. He came to be the light for us"[70]
--Adam Hamilton

"You are going to have the light just a little while longer. Walk while you have the light, before darkness overtakes you. The man who walks in the dark does not know where he is going."
--John 12:35

My wife and I (Dino) pulled into the conference center where I was scheduled to speak for the weekend. We were greeted by our gracious hosts, who led us to the cabin that we would be staying in for the weekend. The beautiful fragrance of the mountainside flowers provided a unique setting for a Bible conference. One of the leaders took us to a cabin and explained to us that it was ours while we were there. The large family room with bunk beds and a large living room seating appeared comfortable. I sensed something was missing. After several hours on the road we both were tired. The leader left the cabin so we could get freshened up for the evening and my wife asked me the question..."Where is the restroom?" Now I knew what was missing. My wife was recovering from a recent surgery and she was not able to walk without some assistance. We went outside and found that the restroom did not appear very far from our cabin. It was in another building. It was a rather winding lane to walk but I thought this is no big deal.

We went to bed and were soundly asleep. My wife and I both woke up around 2 am and we made an executive decision together. We needed to find that path. Since this was prior to flashlights on cell phones, I realized at this early hour that I did not bring a flashlight; therefore

[70] Hamilton, Adam. *John: The Gospel of Light and Life.* Nashville, TN: Abingdon Press, 2015. 18.

we would need to carefully walk the lane from memory. Opening our cabin door brought another reality. The fog combined with the darkness at 2am meant that this would be a challenging journey to arrive at the building with the facilities we needed, it was dark! With masculine authority I told my wife to hold my arm and we started. I thought to myself ..."Is the building right or left"?

As we started down the lane my wife Bobbi sweetly said, "Honey, I think you are going the wrong way." Then with authority she said, "This is not the right way." I am sure that I have been in similar darkness but not in this circumstance. At first we began laughing and then outside howls brought a quiet sobriety to us. This was a dark night. No light anywhere!

I am not sure what total darkness is but this had to be close. Darkness in physics is said to be dark because it absorbs photons. Darkness therefore appears dim compared to other objects.

The darkness is so profound in comparison with everything else. Without light darkness can consume you.

We finally followed my wife's suggestion and found the much needed building we were searching for. When we returned back there was a little opening in the heavens and the appearance of a speck of the moon. We made it back safely and came to a mutual agreement that we would not return to that path leading to the building until daylight and we would request our own personal flashlight for the rest of our stay.

That night of darkness was a complete absence of light. Frankly, it was scary. In the morning as we joined the group for breakfast we were delighted to see the sun breaking through.

Many have written about the light that is needed for our soul. People have written for centuries about the darkness of our souls because of the depravity of our natures. For example, a Spanish mystic known as John of the Cross wrote a poem in the 16th century and did not title it. It became known as The Dark Night. A section of that article states, "Have no fear, take the darkness as your comfort because you are the light shining in the darkness."[71]

"There are several steps in this night, which are related in successive

[71] "Dark Night of the Soul." Wikipedia. February 24, 2019. Accessed April 05, 2019. https://en.wikipedia.org/wiki/Dark_Night_of_the_Soul.

stanzas of the poem. The thesis of the poem is the joyful experience of being guided to God. The only light in this dark night is that which burns in the soul."[72] It appears that some of his images were taken from the writings of Thomas Aquinas and from the writings of Aristotle.

There are forces of darkness everywhere. The spiritual meaning of light is represented by the quality of life we have in Christ. God is light and He gives light. The New Testament declares over and over again that Jesus is the Light. A fascinating verse in the gospel of John declares "*In him was life, and that life was the light of men*" (John 1:4).

There is another dark night. It is again the dark night of the soul. We need the light of Christ. The Scripture in John goes on speaking of the forerunner of Jesus, John the Baptist. "*There was a man sent from God whose name was John. He came as a witness to testify concerning that light, so that through him all might believe. He himself was not the light; he came only as a witness to the light. The true light that gives light to everyone was coming into the world*" (John 1:6-9). John the Baptist was not that light. No one else is! Jesus is that light. No one else can claim it.

Light is a universal and foundational symbol. It was Jesus Himself who said: "*I am the light of the world. Whoever follows me will never walk in darkness, but will have the light of life*" (John 8:12). This statement is the second great "I Am" statement in John. Perhaps the sun was rising and Jesus is comparing Himself to the rising sun. The sun was a symbol of Jehovah God. "*For the LORD God is a sun and shield.*" (Psalms 84:11a). "*But for you who revere my name, the sun of righteousness will rise with healing in its wings* (Malachi 4:2a). The Lord's "*I Am*" statement here also relates to the Feast of Tabernacles. It is that time when the candelabrum is lit in the Temple to remind the people of the guidance of God that directed the people in their wilderness experience.

There are seven occurrences in John where Jesus calls Himself "I am". In the Old Testament when Moses came to a bush that was burning and not consumed, he realized this was a part of his calling to lead the children of Israel from Egypt to the Promise Land. God spoke through the bush and when Moses questioned who would send him the voice was clear..."*I am who I am*". (Exodus 3:14). God is Self-Existent. He doesn't need someone else. He is enough. He is the "*I Am*". Jesus plus

[72] Ibid.

some other light is not what is needed. Jesus is all we need. Jesus was claiming that He is the exclusive source of spiritual light.

Just as a flashlight would be helpful on a dark night to see the way, Jesus is the only way for spiritual light. Plants do not move away from the light. They are positively phototropic; therefore they are drawn to the light. Our souls need a Savior.

I presently live in one of the darkest areas of the United States. Binghamton, New York is usually listed in the top twenty for lack of sunlight.

In the late 1950's my father and I were in Northern New York on vacation. We were avid fishermen. At Black Lake there were some large fish. With huge determination we set out to catch them. Unknown to us a vicious storm was moving in. All of a sudden there was a crack of thunder and we could not see the shoreline. A relative who operated the motor headed the little boat towards what he thought was shore while my Dad insisted he was going the wrong way. Both were wrong. I saw in the distance a flicker of a light. Being a small child I pointed without saying a word. I was petrified. In a matter of minutes we saw the shoreline. My sister put a lantern out, assuming we would stay out too late. Upon our arrival the family gathered around us thanking God we were all right. I was thankful for a sister who put the light out. I believe it saved our lives that night. There is another light. His name is Jesus. When we trust Him as our Savior the dark night of the soul is delivered. I am glad Jesus used that word, Light!

SHOES

"There's 'truth' or 'doctrine' Christianity – these are the folks who write books and preach sermons on who's really a heretic and why their own position is the only correct position on salvation, or drinking, or God's sovereignty. The goal in this camp appears to be to ensure correct doctrine in people's lives. Of course we should care about the truth. But as the Bible itself warns, you can understand all the mysteries and have knowledge, but if you don't have love, you're obnoxious[73].
--John Eldredge

"Your faith has healed you."
--Matthew 9:22

It all started because I wasn't wearing any shoes in church.

I (Jonathan) had a good reason to be walking barefoot through the lobby of the church; I was wearing a Fred Flintstone costume, and as anyone who has seen the classic cartoon is well aware of, Fred never wore shoes.

The purpose of my ridiculous costume was to wish my dad a happy birthday at the end of the service. My sister JoAnna and I made our way unannounced to the podium with a giant bone (with my dad's name Dino written across it) to wish him a happy birthday. Since Fred and Wilma's dog was named Dino in the cartoon it was a perfect way to do something silly and ask a congregation to sing happy birthday to my dad all at the same time.

Everyone in the church laughed and enjoyed the spectacle, except for one member, who met me in the lobby just as I was heading toward the stage. She indignantly declared that I was defaming a holy place (the

[73] Eldredge, John. *The Utter Relief of Holiness.* New York: Faith Words, 2013. 16.

church sanctuary) by not wearing shoes. It seems that for this person my bare feet represented a serious violation of church etiquette.

This person was concerned about keeping the sanctuary a holy place. A place set apart. In the first century Jews were concerned with the same issue. When Jesus enters the Temple during the week before He is crucified, He cleanses the Temple because it had become *"a den of robbers"* (Mark 11:17). Reading this passage could make us assume that proper etiquette in the sanctuary is what Jesus was after.

Some of the first century Jews lived in a world where purity, cleanliness, and etiquette ruled supreme. In fact, they had a long list of actions that could make a person unclean, which would subsequently bar them from entering the Temple area. For this group of people, the goal was purity.

Leviticus 15 lists out a variety of ways a man and woman could be considered unclean and therefore unable to participate in religious ceremonies. Any one man with a bodily discharge (including semen) was considered unclean (15: 1-3). That uncleanliness could spread to others if they touched a bed or sat in a chair that the unclean person touched (4-7), were spit on by an unclean person (8), or used the same cup (12). A woman would be considered unclean during her menstrual period (19). Others would have to take extreme care not to come into contact with anything a woman on her period had touched. Worst of all was sexual relations during a woman's menstrual cycle, which made a person unclean for an entire week (24). This is difficult enough for women, considering the menstrual cycle happens every month, but a woman with any type of blood flow that did not cease was considered continually unclean.

What was the solution to the problem of being unclean? The Torah gives the people a method for transitioning from a state of being unclean to purified, a system of washing and sacrifice (15:13-15, 28-30). A person was not meant to remain continually unclean, and the laws given about clean and unclean in the book of Leviticus are not meant to act as prohibitions or ways to shame others into being labeled as sinners. Rather these purity laws were put in place as a solution for someone who had contracted impurity through regular relationships with other people.[74] The impure person was not considered a "sinner".

[74] Sanders, Ed Parish. *Jesus and Judaism*. London: SCM Press, 2004. 183.

Becoming unclean was not a result of someone committing some sort of sin, impurity was a normal part of the human existence, a regular experience from living with others in community, and therefore the ritual washing and cleansing process was a gracious accommodation from God.

Unfortunately in the first century, some religious leaders began to treat the purity system as a way to separate themselves from others. These normal bodily functions were used to separate people into categories. Those who had become ritually impure were avoided and made to feel sub-human. Better to separate yourself from others who were unclean than to become ritually impure yourself.

Those who were undergoing normal bodily functions were separated into the group of unclean, until the proper time had passed, and an approved sacrifice had been made. However, those who faced medical conditions that were incurable found themselves in a constant state of being impure.

Many readers of the Scriptures today when reading the Old Testament Law consider it to be a means to holiness. This assumption is based on a faulty understanding that following the complex ritual and sacrificial systems of the Old Testament could either save someone, or by their actions they would be declared holy. This idea stems from a faulty reading of Leviticus 19:2 which states: *"...be holy because I, the LORD your God am holy."* If we read the verse carefully, we will notice that it does not say that we are to become holy through actions; rather the verse says that we will be declared holy by God because He is holy. Holiness is not another word for piety, or morality, or following strict rules of cleanliness. Holiness is a declaration from God. God declares something holy and because of that declaration it becomes holy.[75] Holiness is a status that is given to a person or thing, and cannot be revoked or lost because of one's actions. Nothing you can do can make you unholy after God has declared you to be holy.

Further, the Law was never meant to provide a person salvation.[76] Keeping the Law was done in order to act faithfully as part of a covenant

---

[75] Walton John H., and J. Harvey Walton. *Lost World of the Torah*. Downers Grove, IL: Intervarsity Press, 2019. 55-62.

[76] Ibid., 153.

that was made between man and God. The faith required for salvation is the same faith in both the Old and New Testaments.[77] Keeping the Law was simply a way to faithfully reflect God's image into the world (as we are commanded to in Genesis 1:26-27).

What then is a purity system? The Pharisees were a highly politically active group in the first century who recruited others into a system of purity through what they viewed as a strict adherence to the Law in the Old Testament.[78] The Pharisees were consumed with the issue of how to live properly as faithful followers of God in a time of turbulence. Outside forces were in control (the Romans), which they perceived as judgment from God for not being pure enough. They believed if they could just get more people to live as "faithful" Jews following a strict code of purity, then judgment from God would cease and they would be restored.

This view of the Old Testament created an active, powerful, and politically influential group of people who adhered to a strict purity system. In their view, the reason for the suffering of the nation of Israel as a whole was due to those who broke this system of purity. The Pharisees sought to create a community within a community of people who were pure. This of course led to ostracizing others for the sake of their purity (Luke 10:25-37; John 4:1-38).

What is the difference between a holiness system and a purity system? Anything that is declared by God to be holy remains holy. God declared the Ark of the Covenant, Mount Sinai, and the Temple holy.[79] These objects remained holy throughout time because of the declaration of God. A people called holy remain holy regardless of their actions because holiness is not earned.

A purity system like that of the Pharisees seeks to divide people into clean and unclean; welcome and unwelcome. This system caused the Pharisees to miss the entire point of the Law. In Matthew 23 Jesus excoriates the Pharisees because of their blindness to the true purpose

[77] Gundry, Stanley N., ed. *Five Views on Law and Gospel*. Grand Rapids, MI: Zondervan, 1999. 177-199.

[78] Wright, N.T. *Paul and the Faithfulness of God*. Minneapolis, MN: Fortress Press, 2013. 80-90.

[79] Walton & Walton, 2019. 56.

of the Law. *"...you have neglected the more important matters of the law—justice, mercy and faithfulness"* (23:23).

It is into this context that Jesus in Matthew 9 turns the entire system of systematic purity on its head. A woman who had been subject to bleeding for twelve years hears that Jesus is coming through her town. For twelve long years she has sought healing for her issues. She has seen doctor after doctor seeking healing because in her current state, she was forever considered impure. Others would purposely avoid making physical contact with her for fear that then they too would have to wait the prescribed time and undergo the prescribed purity rituals. No one would drink out of the same cup, sit in the same chair, or lay on the same bed as her. When she walked down the street, people would cross to the other side to avoid her. She lived her life rejected, despondent, and helpless, all because of her scars.

When she hears that a rabbi is coming through town that has the power to heal people of infirmities, she sees a glimmer of hope, but that hope is quickly dashed when she realizes that no rabbi would ever actually touch her because in doing so they would become ritually unclean (Luke 10:31). So she thinks to herself, *"If I can only touch his cloak, I will be healed"* (Matthew 9:21).

What was it about Jesus and his cloak that convinced the woman it would contain the power to heal?

In Numbers 15 God tells Moses that the men of Israel should make tassels on the corners of their garments as a reminder of what God had done for them. These tassels were colored blue, the color of heaven to remind the Israelites of their holy calling from on high[80]. Today many Jews wear a prayer shawl reminiscent of these tassels that were to be attached to the cloaks of all observant Jews.

These fringes are referenced by the prophet Malachi. *"The sun of righteousness will rise with healing in its wings"* (Malachi 4:2). The Hebrew word for wings is the same word that is used to describe the corners of a person's cloak in Numbers 15.[81] This prophecy led some to

[80] Phillips, John. *Exploring the Gospel of Matthew: An Expository Commentary.* Grand Rapids, MI: Kregel, 2005. 168.

[81] Bell, Rob. *Velvet Elvis: Repainting the Christian Faith.* Grand Rapids, MI: Zondervan, 2005, 106.

believe that when the Messiah came, even his cloak would possess the powers of God to heal those with infirmities.

Based on this ancient promise, the woman reaches out in the crowd and touches the corner of Jesus' garment. This action of course would have made Jesus ceremonial impure, and he would have been expected to go through the ritual practice of cleansing and sacrifice before he could resume normal social contact. In fact as she pushes through the crowd, everyone that she came into contact with was now considered unclean.[82]

But something strange and unexpected happens here. Instead of her infecting Jesus, Jesus somehow infects her. He turns to her and says, "*...take heart daughter... your faith has healed you*" (Matthew 9:22). What causes this sudden societal change? What gives Jesus the right to subvert societal norms of clean and unclean?

If we take a moment to read all of Matthew chapter 9, we will see Jesus coming into contact with almost every category of people who were considered unclean: those with disabilities (1-2), tax collectors and sinners (9-12), gluttons (14), dead bodies (24-25), the blind (27), and the demon-possessed (32-34). Every single one of these people would have been considered unclean and people to be avoided. But Jesus doesn't avoid them, he welcomes them, he engages with them, he reaches out and touches them. The Pharisees are so offended by the actions of Jesus that they declare him to be working for the prince of demons (Matthew 9:34).

Why is Jesus doing this?

Jesus in this passage is reflecting God's promise from the Old Testament. What God has declared holy retains its holiness regardless of the view of others. Holiness is something that is granted based on a decree from God, not based on our ability to live up to others expectations.

In the first century the characters Jesus interacts with in Matthew 9 would all have been considered outsiders, unclean, impure, and people to be avoided. People with disabilities, those who cheated others for financial gain, those who eat or drink too much, people deemed

[82] Wright, Nicholas Thomas. *Matthew for Everyone.* Louisville, KY: Westminster John Knox Press, 2004. 105.

undesirable physically, and even people so far gone that they are considered possessed by the devil.

The Pharisees would go to great lengths to avoid all of these people because they would be considered impure. Instead of seeing people as created by God and declared holy, they looked at others with contempt because they did not meet their standard of purity. But Jesus is different, instead of seeing these individuals as unclean, impure, or dangerous, Jesus sees them as people in need of love, because for Jesus, people are more important than labels, and people are more important that purity rituals.

We have all felt the sting of being rejected. The church has sadly excluded some from membership because instead of seeing everyone as a beautiful reflection of the image of God, all we can see are those things that make them impure in our sight. But Jesus doesn't look at any of these people as impure, the people that others avoided He specifically reaches out and touches. He takes them into His arms and welcomes them and declares them holy. Holiness is a declaration by God about someone that cannot be taken away.

How does Jesus see you? As someone that is impure because of transgressions. Are you a failure because others have rejected you? Ostracized because you don't fit into what others find acceptable?

When Jesus looks at you He declares you holy. And nothing you can do can change that.

CHILDREN

"We have exchanged love of family and home for cyber friends and living in constant motion that robs the soul from memories- and perhaps from that still, small voice that longs to be heard."[83]
--Billy Graham

"Let the little children come to me"
--Matthew 19:14

EVERY YEAR SEVERAL MILLION CHILD ABUSE CASES ARE REPORTED IN AMERICA. Child abuse can result from physical, emotional, and sexual harm that has been perpetrated on the child. As I (Dino) traveled into Africa several years ago, I saw a young child who continually stared at me. Every time I looked to him he looked away. I soon discovered the reason; he had been abused and could not look at men.

As a pastor for many years I had the experience of sitting with families in my role as pastor. From the appearance of the children and their body language it was at times obvious that something was going on, there were times when through this process we discovered that child abuse was the cause of this behavior.

From religious leaders to the wealthy, and poor there are cases of child abuse. Researchers have done studies on the result of child abuse. It clearly adversely affects individuals into adulthood. From family violence to childhood neglect, abuse raises its ugly head for many victims. Many experience disorders and adverse experiences in adulthood because of child abuse.

There are many images of Jesus Christ. He is the savior, healer,

[83] "10 Quotes from Billy Graham on Family - The Billy Graham Library Blog." The Billy Graham Library. December 21, 2018. Accessed February 23, 2019. https://billygrahamlibrary.org/blog-10-quotes-from-billy-graham-on-family/.

forgiver, leader, servant, and on and on it goes, but seldom do we focus on His love and compassion for children. Other than the occasional Sunday school lessons to children, we hear little of His love of and attitude towards, children. Unfortunately we often hear of clergy abuse of the children.

In Matthew 19:13-15 we find the little children are brought to Jesus to have his hands laid on them and to pray for them. The disciples of our Lord rebuked the people. The word that is used here is from the Greek word '*epitimao*'. It is the same word that is used when Jesus rebuked evil spirits (Matthew 17:18). The word is a rebuke that is undeserved. When Jesus rebuked the evil spirits they deserved it, but when the disciples rebuked the children they did not deserve it. The context makes it very clear that Jesus wanted the children to come to Him. The word 'come' is a verb that means to 'go' or 'come'. He is saying in essence, 'Don't stop them.' The word child is from a noun that means infants and children. Jesus is saying that He does not want them to be blocked from seeing him.

My granddaughter, Olivia, recently performed in the Broadway production, "Fiddler on the Roof". When I saw her come on the stage my eyes were fixated on her. After the show there was a gathering as the cast departed from backstage. While I enjoyed all the performers, I wanted to see my granddaughter and whether she came to me or I went to her I was going to give her a big hug. The idea is that I would not be detained nor would I want someone to rebuke neither her nor me. That is the meaning of the word 'come'. Notice the children were brought to Him. Jesus says do not 'hinder them'. He wants the people to know that to forbid the children to come to Him is to prevent them from what is best for a child.

The emphasis that Jesus addresses is that these little children are 'of such'. In other words they are what the Kingdom of God is like. This is a powerful thought that Jesus is communicating. It is in the possessive case which opens up numerous purposes. The kingdom is childlike, or the kingdom is for the children. All Christians are called children and grandchildren of the kingdom of God. The word translated as kingdom is speaking to the realm of God's kingdom. When one speaks about the realm of a kingdom or the king, the reference is to the authority of a leader and His sovereign right to execute His plans and purposes.

Jesus then laid hands on the children and went away. This event is probably one the children will remember the rest of their years on earth. This is a lesson for all, especially the apostles, to see.

Christian parents have a wonderful privilege and opportunity. In the world that we live in today society is becoming more and more secular. Parents need to be careful to protect their children from abuse but also need to deepen their faith with consistent study and understanding of God's Word. Children will ask questions like: "Why does a good God allow evil?" "What is the evidence for the existence of God?" "Why would a God of love allow people to go to hell?" "How do we know that Jesus rose from the grave?" "Is the Bible accurate since it is so old and has gone through so many language changes?" "What does the Bible say about slavery, racism, sacrifice of flesh, homosexuality", and on and on.

With so many questions, parents need help. The church needs to be a safe haven for children and teenagers. Schools need to be places which at the very least will not tear down the belief system of parents. There needs to be a sense of calm and spiritual help in the home. Questions will come up. Children need to be able to express themselves. Parents need to study the Bible with their children.

Complaints and criticism of the church will eventually teach children to either distrust the church, or people where they worship, or the parents who are disagreeing with the church. It is wise for parents to ask their children about their faith and if they are able to accept the truth. I am a parent. I don't even pretend to have all the answers. However, I do want my children to know I love them and when they fail, Dad is there to advise, correct, help, engage, and especially love them.

Child abuse, it is a difficult subject.

Since I travel frequently, I've been on too many airplanes. I am always glad to arrive home. Recently I entered a terminal and there was an amazing raucous. A young boy was screaming at his mother, refusing to get off the floor. His father came out of the men's rest room and settled the disruption. He kicked his son in the head. I thought to myself if I were that child I would be unconscious. How tragic.

Abuse seems to be everywhere. Jesus said that we were to let the children come to Him. Our children, above all, need Jesus. Our children need to know heroes and those who are courageous for Christ. C.S.

Lewis said, "Since it is so likely that children will meet cruel enemies, let them at least have heard of brave knights and heroine courage."[84]

"Children" is a word that should remind us of the love and graciousness of Jesus, and how He welcomed them into his arms.

[84] Lewis C.S. *On Stories and Other Literature* 1966 C.S. Lewis Daily.

4-OUT-UP

"Baptized in the river
I've seen a vision of my life and I want to be delivered
In the city was a sinner
I've done a lot of things wrong but I swear I'm a believer
Like the prodigal son, I was out on my own
Now I'm trying to find my way back home
Baptized in the river
I'm delivered, I'm delivered"[85]
--Good Charlotte

"He was lost and is found"
--Luke 15:32

"Hike!"

That was my (Jonathan) signal to run four steps forward as quickly as I could, then plant, pivot, and twist my entire body towards the sideline. The cut towards the sideline was the most important move of the entire play. It was here that I would look back to the quarterback as if I was ready to receive the ball, with my hands outstretched to catch a pass. The defender would assume the ball was coming my way and would try and step in front of me to block or intercept the pass. At that very moment I would make an immediate turn up the field. The brief moment in which my defender was still moving towards the sideline was the precise instant that the ball would come my way, not towards the sideline, but towards the end zone. If I executed the fake well, I would be open, running towards the end zone with the ball making its way to me for a touchdown.

[85] Charlotte, Good, writer. "The River." In *Good Morning Revival*. Msi Music Corp, 2007.

My favorite play is ingrained in my memory. As one of 4 children in our family, I can clearly remember some of the epic battles that took place in our backyard. My siblings and I would gather in the yard after school to play football, with my dad being the full time quarterback. Regardless of the fact that we were children, and the quarterback threw most passes underhanded, these games turned into epic battles that lasted until my mom called us in for dinner. Around the dinner table that night, we would either brag about our victory or decry the unfairness of our defeat. At a young age the rivalry between me and my brothers and sister was established. As soon as you were old enough to run, you were out on the field of play competing with one another.

4 – out – up. That was my secret play. At the most important moments of our backyard games my father would look at me, and simply say those three magic words: 4 – out – up.

Today as an adult I am sure my father didn't keep my play a secret. I'm sure that my siblings probably tried to run that play on me a few times, and I'm sure it was successful. But as a kid I felt like I was in on a special secret, a special play that gave me an advantage over everyone else in our backyard football games.

If you have more than one child or grew up in a family with siblings, you can relate. Beating a member of your family means that you have bragging rights around the dinner table. Regardless of the type of relationship, we can all certainly relate to the feeling of winning a competition over someone else.

In Luke 15 we find the story of the prodigal son. Despite this story only occurring once in all four gospels, it has become one of the most well-known stories of Jesus. In Luke, Jesus finishes off a series of parables about things that are lost, beginning with a lost sheep (1-7), a lost coin (8-10), and concluding with a lost son (11-32).

The story is both simple and profound. A son comes to his father asking for his share of the family estate. The father, without reservation, gives the son his rightful share of all that he has. My father shared a special play with me, but this son wants everything from the father. The lost son then embarks on a journey to a distant land where he squanders all that his father has given him, which results in the son living in poverty and longing for the comforts of his father's home. Realizing his mistake, the lost son embarks on the journey back home, hoping that his father will give him a small measure of mercy and allow him to live as an indentured servant because even that lowly level of existence is certainly better than starving to death in a foreign land. Upon his return the father is overjoyed to see his lost son. The father embraces the son, and he throws a party for the entire town to celebrate the return of his lost son.

It is hard for us to read this story today and not see the father as a stand in for God, and us as the prodigal. I have personally heard many sermons on this passage, and most of them follow a familiar pattern of meaning: no matter how far you have strayed from God, he is always willing to welcome you back into his arms, because he is a loving and forgiving God. This application is true, and the passage can certainly be seen as a story of the forgiveness of God. But if you take a step back and consider the story again in terms of what the first audience would have heard in the story, a whole new avenue for understanding opens up.

The story begins with a simple statement from Jesus.

> "*There was a man who had two sons*" (Luke 15:11).

For the Jews in the first century, the beginning of this story would have brought to mind stories from their history where a man had two sons.[86] In Genesis 4 we learn of the first father, Adam, and his two sons, Cain and Abel. Cain the firstborn and Abel his younger brother are almost immediately thrust into a competition because of the sacrifices that they bring to God. "*Now Abel kept flocks, and Cain worked the soil*" (4:2). God looks upon the sacrifice that Abel brings with favor, but He is displeased with the sacrifice that Cain offers. The reasoning behind God's acceptance of one sacrifice and the rejection of the other is not mentioned in the text, but the result is that Cain is exceedingly jealous of Abel. His jealousy becomes so inflamed that Cain commits the first murder in the Biblical account by attacking and killing his brother Abel in a field (4:8). Adam had two sons, jealousy ensues, and one of his sons murders the other.

Adam, the father of all mankind, had two sons.

---

[86] Levine, Amy-Jill. *Short Stories by Jesus: The Enigmatic Parables of a Controversial Rabbi*. New York NY: Harper Collins, 2015.

In Genesis 21 we find the story of Abraham. Abraham who was to become the father of the nation of Israel finds himself without an heir. Abraham is promised by God that one day he will indeed have a son, even though he has passed the age where fathering a child would have been considered possible (Genesis 17:1-2; 21:2). Before this son of promise is conceived, Abraham's wife, Sarah, tells Abraham to conceive a child with her maidservant, Hagar, so that Abraham's family line will continue. Abraham conceives a child with Hagar and names the son Ishmael. Abraham's first born son is described this way: *"He will be a wild donkey of a man; his hand will be against everyone and everyone's hand against him, and he will live in hostility toward all his brothers"* (Genesis 16:12). Abraham soon after is able to conceive a son with Sarah whom he names Isaac, which makes for an odd family dynamic. Abraham now has two sons from two different women. At the birth of Ishmael, it is confirmed to him that these two brothers will live in a constant state of rivalry.

Sarah soon regrets her decision to allow Abraham to conceive with Hagar and asks that her maidservant and Ishmael be sent away to a distant land (Genesis 21). Hagar and Ishmael are sent away, and the older son of Abraham becomes an outcast, while the younger son goes on to become the son of promise (21:12).

The father of the nation of Israel, Abraham, had two sons.

Isaac does not learn from his father's mistakes. Isaac and his wife, Rebekah, are barren exactly as his father Abraham was. Isaac prays to God and is blessed with not only one son, but two. Twins are to be born to Isaac and Rebekah; however the author of Genesis tells us that, "*...the older will serve the younger*" (Gen 25:23). Two boys are born to Isaac and are named Jacob and Esau. Esau is born first and is followed by Jacob. Unfortunately, the antagonism between these two sons extends not just between them, but between their parents as well. Isaac loves Esau more than Jacob, and Rebekah loves Jacob more than Esau (25:28). This rivalry comes to a climax one day when Jacob convinces Esau to sell his birthright (or special blessing passed on from the father to the son) for a bowl of stew. The younger son steals the blessing from the older brother, continuing the pattern of sibling rivalry (Genesis 27:41-43).

Isaac the son of Abraham, the child of promise, had two sons.

As Jesus begins his story of two sons in Luke 15, his original hearers would immediately be reminded of their history. When a father has more than one son, rivalry ensues. In each of these stories, like most of our modern day narratives, the stories have a hero and a villain. One will be the son of promise; the other rejected and subjected to punishment. In Isaac's case, one son will serve the other, or in the case of Cain and Abel, one will murder the other. Jesus' audience would immediately recognize this pattern, and would have attempted to fit each son into these prescribed molds. With this in mind it is easy to assume that in Luke 15 the younger son who asks for his father's inheritance and squanders it in a foreign country is the villain in the story. The younger son is simply following in the footsteps of Cain, Ishmael, and Esau. The first hearers would not be surprised to learn of the desperate situation of the younger son after he had squandered all of his father's wealth:

> *"He longed to fill his stomach with the pods that the pigs were eating, but no one gave him anything"* (Luke 15:16).

Lost, destitute, and starving in a foreign land. This situation would have been a familiar position for the entire nation of Israel, who throughout their history had found themselves in an eerily similar situation.[87] As a nation they had rejected God, only to find themselves living out the story of the younger son. They were given the Law, and the prophets, the blessing of God only to squander it with unrighteous living, which resulted them being prisoners in a foreign land because of their decisions.

Jesus original audience would have heard the story as a clear reference to these ancient Hebrew stories. In the Old Testament when a man has two sons, one son will be chosen over the other for blessing or favor. In the story of the lost son in Luke 15, the audience would immediately understand who the hero in the story was and who the villain was.

The younger son, who asks for his inheritance while his father is still alive, is in essence saying to his father that the money is more important to him than time with his father. The story of the lost son stands in stark contrast to Deuteronomy 21, where the people of Israel are commanded to stone a son who is rebellious and will not obey his father (21:21). This

[87] Wright, N.T. *Jesus and the Victory of God*. Minneapolis: Fortress Press, 1997. 127.

passage also gives commands to a man who has two wives who bear him sons. If a man has two sons from two different wives (one from the wife he loves, and one from the wife he does not love) the firstborn son is to receive a double share of inheritance even if that son is born from the unloved wife (21:17). In the ancient world the firstborn son received an extra benefit. When Jesus tells this story, he seems to have this passage in the back of his mind, but the story of the lost son will not follow this same pattern because in this story it is the younger son who receives an inheritance before the older son.[88]

His squandering of the money in a foreign land only adds to the caricature of the younger son being the villain in the story. If you were asked which son you wanted to emulate, the obvious answer would be the son of promise, and the one who stayed faithful to the father. When the lost son finally comes to his senses and returns to his father, we are shocked to see the incredible graciousness of the father welcoming his son back into the family. If that were the end of the parable, the choice would be clear. We should be grateful for our father in heaven because He is always willing to welcome us back into the fold no matter what we have done. His grace and mercy abound even for those who have rejected him outright. There is always a place at the table of fellowship for a lost son. If a man has two sons, we should be like the older son, who worked faithfully in his father's house. But the story does not end there; Jesus puts a twist on the end of the story that changes everything.

A man had two sons.

To celebrate the return of his lost son, the father orders that a fatted calf be killed. A fatted calf would have fed the entire village.[89] This was not a simple small celebration of the return of the younger son with immediate family; this was a community wide event. The father's actions here go against everything we expect to happen to a wayward son. The son, if he is welcomed back at all, should expect to live a life of remorse and regret humbling himself by serving in his father's household for his indiscretions.

The entire thrust of the parable is about turning expectations upside

---

[88] Evans, Craig A. *Luke*. Edited by W. Ward. Gasque. Peabody, MA: Hendrickson Publishers, 1990. 234.

[89] Wright, 1997. 129.

down. Jesus tells this story to confront the original hearers with a choice, which son are you? Midway through the story the choice would have been obvious, the lost son has dishonored the family, and the older son has acted righteously and should therefore be an example for us to follow. But Luke adds an addendum to the story that seems to change everything.

Up to this point the older son has done absolutely nothing wrong. The entire community would be aware of the younger son's indiscretion. Imagine the gossip that would have ensued when the younger son demanded his inheritance only to squander it in a foreign land with "wild living" (15:13).[90] As a community member who attended the celebration of the return of the son, you would have been well aware of why the son went missing. The chatter that surrounded his former way of life would have spread through the town like wildfire, and the actions of the father would have surprised everyone. Certainly others would have evaluated their own willingness to accept such a wayward son back into the fold.

Would those in the audience have been willing to forgive their own flesh and blood? Was all this expense warranted? Is the unfaithful son even worthy of such a reception? What a fool the father is, his son stole everything from him before and now he is here to do it again. Plenty of time would have been spent evaluating both the wayward son, and the father who foolishly and lavishly welcomed him back.

Imagine for a moment how the reputation of the older son would have been elevated in comparison with his younger brother. The unspoken level of respect the community would have for a son who, in sharp contrast to his foolish brother, stayed faithful to his family and his work. Instead of the instant gratification of momentary pleasure like his foolish younger brother, the elder son recognized the benefit of long term faithfulness.

A man had two sons, a lost son and a faithful son.

Luke goes on to describe the mercy of the father and the celebration that ensued from the return of the lost son. With a blatant disregard for any criticism that would fall on him, the father kills the fatted calf, and the party begins. The celebration captivated the entire village. Food and

---

[90] Ibid., 133.

drink are offered liberally, and the entire community is now celebrating riotously the return of the lost son. It is at this point that the reader is alerted to the fact that something is missing.

> *"Meanwhile, the older son was in the field. When he came near the house, he heard music and dancing. So he called one of the servants and asked him what was going on. Your brother has come, he replied and your father has killed the fattened calf because he has him back safe and sound. The older brother became angry and refused to go in. So his father went out and pleaded with him"* (Luke 15:25-28).

What Jesus does here in this parable is to save the shocking revelation for the end. At this point His hearers are putting themselves in the shoes of the older son. In this parable Jesus is telling a story about how God is acting in history. The story is not just about a man with two sons, it is the story of the nation of Israel. The people of Israel would recognize their own sordid history of turning away from the one true God and consorting with other gods (Amos 2:4-5). The story of the lost son is their story as the lost nation. Thankfully, God is acting in the here and now to bring all of those lost people under His wing, welcoming them back into the family with a celebration of restoration. But where is the older son during this celebration? He is conspicuously absent from the party.

One of the interesting questions that we should immediately ask is: why was the older brother unaware of the celebration? If a community wide event was going on, why would the elder son be surprised to find that his lost brother had returned and that he had somehow missed out on the party? And how could the father have seemingly forgotten his oldest son? Did he somehow forget that he was indeed the father of two sons? The older son seems totally unaware that his father has chosen to kill a fattened calf that belongs to the older brother, he seems unaware of the return of his brother, and he does not seem to be invited to the celebration for his lost brother's return. The original hearers might have jumped to the conclusion that we are seeing another father make the mistake of favoring one son over the other just as their forefathers had done. (Genesis 25).

The older son is excluded from the party. While others are celebrating with food and drink, the older son is outside the house, refusing to attend the party. The older son should be engaged in celebration, but instead he chooses to exclude himself from the festivities.

We never find the father asking his younger unfaithful son any of the questions that we would want to know the answer to. How much of the inheritance is left? How did you spend all of the fortune? Where were you for all of the time that you were away? Even when he is asked for a share of the inheritance, the father never asks why, nor does he ever seem to consider declining his son's request. We also do not see the older son ask any of the questions that we would certainly ask: How much of my inheritance is left now that my younger brother has squandered so much of our family wealth? If my brother has taken his inheritance, what is to stop me from asking for mine as well?

And yet despite these contrasts at the end of the parable it is the younger son who is celebrated while the older son is left outside in judgment (Matthew 25:30). What has the older son done to deserve this? The father gives us the answer at the end of the parable.

> *"My son, the father said, you are always with me, and everything I have is yours"* (Luke 15:31).

The older son was now the rightful owner of the father's entire kingdom, all of the family land, resources, and belongings are now rightfully his. So why is the brother on the outside looking in on the celebration? Why is he not attending the party where there is food, drink, and merriment?

The older brother missed out because he did not recognize that all things in his father's kingdom were already his. Jesus tells this story to not only emphasize the willingness of God to forgive those who have gone astray, but also to remind his hearers that everything is already theirs. They do not have to struggle and strive for forgiveness, it already belongs to them. God is not holding back anything; it is rather our refusal to recognize that everything is already ours that leads to us placing ourselves under judgment. We are on the outside looking in like the older brother, not because we have been excluded from anything; rather we exclude ourselves by refusing to accept the outlandish and generous promises of God.

Where is the party for the older son? Where is his fatted calf? Where is his share of the inheritance that he has rightly earned?

All of it already belonged to him. The entire kingdom, the entire inheritance all belonged to him. The land, food, houses, cattle, everything his eyes could see, already belonged to him.

What does this teach us?

The older brother was not kicked out of the party, he was already in. The father in this story does not have a guest list, everyone is invited. The party is not exclusive; the entire village is taking part regardless of name, stature, or personal history. The father's generosity extends not only to his son, to whom he lavishes forgiveness and acceptance, but to the entire town.

The party took place in the older son's rightful home, the fatted calf that was prepared was part of his inheritance, and the entire celebration was funded with resources that belonged to him. The older brother is excluded from the celebration because he failed to recognize that inclusion came before exclusion. He chose to exclude himself when everything already belonged to him. How often in our own lives do we behave like the older brother? We stand on the sidelines missing out on the relentless love of God because we assume God has a guest list on which our names may or may not appear. Or even worse we assume we are on the inside of that party and take pleasure in those whose names we believe are not on the list. Sadly, we may at times actually take pleasure in someone else being excluded.

In the story of the prodigal son, the reception for the lost son represents more than just his homecoming. The party is the offer of forgiveness and fellowship with God that we all long for. The party represents our eternal life with God, and the twist in the parable is not just that everyone is invited, but that everyone is already in.

In this parable we see grace and forgiveness, but we also see judgment. Judgment in the parables of Jesus often times operates in this way: we are not excluded because God keeps us out of the party, but we are excluded because we choose to exile ourselves. Like the older brother, we have every right to be at a celebration in our own home, but we fail to recognize that everything is already ours. We obsess over what others are doing, we question whether or not someone else deserves to be sitting at a place of restoration, and all the while we forget that everything already belongs to us. Robert Farrar Capon explains the idea of this parable in this way referring to the difference between those on the inside of the party and those on the outside:

> "The difference between heaven and hell, accordingly, is simply that those in heaven accept the endless forgiveness, while those in hell reject it. Indeed, the precise hell of hell is its endless refusal to open the door to the reconciled and reconciling party that stands forever on its porch and knocks, equally, endlessly, for permission to bring in the Supper of the Lamb (Revelation 3:20)."[91]

Inclusion comes before exclusion. Forgiveness is already ours. The lost son simply needed to accept the forgiveness that was already given by the father. When he returned home he did not have to say a word, forgiveness had already been granted. The lost son assumed that he was excluded by the father only to find that upon his return that he was never on the outside. The older son was the rightful owner of everything, including the food and drink used at the celebration, but he missed the party because he did not recognize his position. Everything the father had was already his.

Both of the sons misunderstood the nature of the father's love. The younger son assumed that the fathers love would be taken away because of his unfaithfulness. The older son assumed that his behavior was somehow earning the father's love. But this story of Jesus tells us that the father's love cannot be earned or lost, it simply has to be accepted regardless of what we have done.

In his book *The Great Divorce*, C.S. Lewis speaks of the choices we make in relation to eternity:

> "There are only two kinds of people in the end: those who say to God, 'Thy will be done,' and those to whom God says, in the end, 'Thy will be done.' All that are in

[91] Capon, Robert Farrar. *The Parables of Judgment*. Grand Rapids, MI: Eerdmans, 1993. 14.

> hell choose it. Without that self-choice there could be no hell. No soul that seriously and constantly desires joy will ever miss it. Those who seek find. To those who knock it is opened.'"[92]

The older brother had access to all the promises and benefits of the father, yet he chose to live outside of the party, outside of the fellowship, outside in darkness because he could not accept what already belonged to him. The forgiveness of the father, the fatted calf, the houses, the riches, all belonged to him. His invitation to the party was not lost; he simply chose not to attend.

In this parable and other stories in the New Testament, judgment, sometimes referred to as hell, or being excluded, or being outside in darkness, comes not because God has excluded us, but rather because we have excluded ourselves from his love. The father in the parable of the lost son is generous, forgiving, and lavishes love on both of his sons, and yet only one of his sons ever really accepts this grace.

As a child I assumed that I had secret knowledge of an unstoppable play in our backyard football games. The reality was that the play was available to all of my siblings.

4 – out – up are words from my childhood that bring to mind a special secret play.

In this parable judgment is not an act of the father excluding the older son. Judgment comes upon the older son because he refused to accept what was already his. The difference between the two sons in this parable is simply their willingness to accept and enjoy what already belonged to them.

A man had two sons, which one are you?

[92] Lewis, C. S. *The Great Divorce: A Dream*. New York: Harper One, HarperCollins, 2007. 75.

IMAGE

"There was a human being in the first century who was called 'Divine,' 'Son of God,' 'God,' and 'God from God,' whose titles were 'Lord,' 'Redeemer,' 'Liberator,' and 'Savior of the World'. Who was that person? Before Jesus ever existed, all those terms belong to Caesar Augustus. To proclaim them of Jesus the Christ was thereby to deny them of Caesar the Augustus."[93]
--John Dominic Crossan

"The Son is the radiance of God's glory and the exact representation of his being."
--Hebrews 1:3

IT STARTED WITH A BOTTLE OF WATER AND A SOFT PLACE IN THE GRASS TO sit. From there that kindness was transformed into a tantrum, and ended with a police escort.

In 2016 I (Jonathan) attended a political rally with my wife for one of the Presidential candidates. Living in Florida means that we get plenty of visits from potential representatives, so on a Tuesday night in October we hopped in the car and drove the twenty minutes to a park near Fort Lauderdale to witness one of the final rallies of the election season. One of the rules of political rallies is that the candidate is always late. Campaigns are trying to squeeze in every possible appearance with prospective voters, and by mid-morning they are hopelessly behind schedule. By the time they arrive at the last stop of the day the candidate is sometimes over an hour late. This night was no exception.

At the time my wife was seven months pregnant with our son William, but she insisted that the opportunity to see a possible future president paled in comparison to the discomfort she would have to deal

[93] Crossan, John D. *God & Empire, Jesus Against Rome, Then and Now.* New York, NY: Harper One, 2008, 24.

with. As we made our way towards the stage, we chose a spot just in front of the line of TV cameras to wait for the rally to begin.

The air buzzed with anticipation, every so often people would crane their necks expecting the candidate to arrive, and excitement would ripple through the crowd, only to die out when we realized the candidate had yet to arrive. The wait began to drag on; and soon the candidate was an hour behind schedule, then ninety minutes. Our patience was being tested. But our conviction that our support at the rally would be a part of a larger movement kept us in place.

As we stood there and waited, a man next to us kindly offered my wife a bottle of water. It was a warm Florida evening, and she graciously accepted the offer. He then offered us a place to sit next to him, which was also graciously accepted. Almost a full hour later, the program finally began. Local politicians opened the rally, followed by members of Congress who gave their glowing endorsement of the candidate for the upcoming election. With each speaker the applause from the crowd grew, knowing that the climax of the night would be a speech from the person everyone in the crowd wanted to be the next President of the United States.

When the candidate finally took the stage the crowd erupted in cheers, shouts of joy erupted, and there was a feeling that everyone in this small park was somehow united to a singular cause. We were all there to unite behind a singular vision, and on election night we would be victorious.

About ten minutes into the speech I heard a commotion from the crowd, at first I thought it was another group chant starting, praising the candidate. Every so often a chant of support would rise from the crowd heaping praise on our future leader. A moment later I turned my head to see the man next to us that had kindly given us the bottle of water and a place to sit. His entire demeanor had changed. Moments ago he was a fellow supporter, one of us, those united for a common cause; he was on the right side of this battle fighting with us to the bitter end to win the political battle. He was even kind enough to offer my wife a bottle of water and a place to sit. Now his face was red, and he was screaming at the top of his lungs.

I was shocked to see that he had torn open his shirt to reveal another shirt underneath on which was an image of the candidate where he had scrawled accusatory words. He ranted and raved trying to drown out the candidate speaking from the stage with his protest. Spit flew from his mouth, his arms waved as if they were completely out of his control, he had transformed from a kind fellow supporter of the cause to a raving lunatic.

Thankfully, security officers quickly descended on the situation and escorted the man out of the park. I was shocked both by the man's outburst, and wondered, would that sort of behavior be effective? Did he or anyone else think that screaming, yelling, and resorting to disruption would actually change the minds of anyone in the park? Why would he brave the traffic to the event, the security check, and sit on the grass in the park on a warm Florida night for over 90 minutes only to immediately be thrown out after his outburst?

Clearly this man was not a fellow supporter. His vision for the future of America was quite different than ours, and his chosen way to communicate that was through loud and obnoxious protest. Politics can unite us or divide us. A strong leader can inspire the masses for good, or animate others for resistance. The political party that you identify with should reflect your values. Your politics are a reflection of you as a person and what you value. My wife and I were at the political rally because we both felt that this particular candidate would best reflect our values.

In the first century, what political party you ascribed to was a very clear dividing line between you and others. There were several political options for you to choose from at this time. One option was to cooperate with the ruling power of the day. The Romans had conquered most of the known world at the time, so joining in with their cause meant that you would be on the side of the victors. Others would resist the empire. Deep in their hearts they knew that the Romans were unworthy rulers, and they resisted until the day a leader would rise up, rally supporters and restore the fortunes of the faithful.

In America, election years cause great division. In the gospel of Matthew Jesus is asked a question that forces Him to wade into the dangerous waters of politics.

> *"Then the Pharisees went out and laid plans to trap him in his words. They sent their disciples to him along with*

> *the Herodians. 'Teacher,' they said, We know you are a man of integrity and that you teach the way of God in accordance with the truth. You aren't swayed by men, because you pay no attention to who they are. Tell us then, what is your opinion? Is it right to pay taxes to Caesar or not'? But Jesus, knowing their evil intent, said, 'You hypocrites, why are you trying to trap me! Show me the coin used for paying the tax.' They brought him a denarius, and he asked them, 'Whose portrait is this? And whose inscription? ' Caesar's they replied. Then he said to them, 'Give to Caesar what is Caesar's, and to God what is God's.' When they heard this they were amazed so they left him and went away"* Matthew 22:15-22.

Jesus is confronted by two opposing factions. The Pharisees in the first century were a sect of Jews who sought the restoration of the nation of Israel through strict adherence to the Law. The Herodians were a political group in the first century that backed the Roman Empire and the ruler Herod. These two opposing groups joined together in this passage to trap Jesus with a difficult question about paying taxes. To fully appreciate Jesus response to this question we must first understand why this question was so divisive. To understand the question and Jesus' answer in light of the context of the day, we need to go back to the beginning. This question is not just about taxes, but whose image society would be made to reflect.

In Genesis 1 the culmination of the creative process of God takes place on day six, where God creates mankind. Man is the only part of the creation that has the special designation of being created in the image of God.

> *"Then God said, Let us make man in our image, in our likeness…"* Genesis 1:26.

Human beings are said to be in the likeness or image of God. But being in the image of God does not entail physical resemblance; an image reflects the character of God into the world.

First and foremost gender and sexuality are a part of what God has created; they are not part of the creator.[94] The idea of likeness does not extend to whether God is male or female. God is a Spirit (John 4:24) and therefore not confined by gender norms. Likeness here is a mode of representation.

The Genesis story is about God creating our known world, but the story also operates as God building a holy place in which He will reside. The creation story of Genesis operates as God building His Temple. The earth, skies, water, and animals are all participants in this holy place, this is why God declares His creation to be "good" (Genesis 1:10, 12, 18, 21, 25, 31). The world created by God in Genesis 1-2 functions as the Temple or dwelling place for God. A Temple in this case is not simply a building; it is the place where God will take up residence. The entire earth functions as the residence or holy place for God to exist in. God is creating a space where He will rule, all of the created order is made for His enjoyment. However, in this created order only one aspect is said to reflect the image of God.

> *"So God created man in his own image, in the image of God he created him..."* (Genesis 1:27).

Whenever human beings construct a Temple or holy place the culminating action is to place an image in that temple that represents the God you will be worshipping. As God finishes creation He creates humans in His image. The purpose of humans is to reflect God into the world, because God is not physically present.

Many holy places today have within them representations of divine beings. If you were to enter a church on a Sunday morning you would likely not be surprised to find a cross or even a picture of Jesus in the sanctuary. We understand that these images are not gods, but rather visual representations that help us in worship. By looking at the cross I am reminded of the sacrifice of Christ, the cross is a pathway that leads me in the direction of the divine. That path is not divine (I would certainly not pray and believe the cross would suddenly animate and

---

[94] Longman, Tremper, and Scot Mcknight. *Genesis.* Grand Rapids: Zondervan, 2016.

answer my prayer), rather it is an image that reflects what God has done in the world.

Man is made in the image of God and is placed in God's creation Temple in order to reflect God into the world. We are God's image because we are to be the ones that represent God on this earth. Much like an image in a Temple would remind worshipers that the gods were active in the world, so God placed us in His Temple (creation) to be a reflection of Him in the world. When the work of building a Temple is completed and things have settled down, God takes up His rest in the Temple to begin the daily administration of His new world (Genesis 2:2-3). John Walton explains the role of the seventh day of rest in this way:

> *"The role of the temple in the ancient world is not primarily a place for people to gather in worship like modern churches. It is a place for the deity—a sacred space. It is his home, but more importantly his headquarters – the control room. When the deity rests in the temple it means that he is taking, command that he is mounting to his throne to assume his rightful place and his proper role."*[95]

In this way we are in God's image. Not that someone could look at us and decide that we remind them of God because of our appearance, but rather we are God's image in the world. If we are living properly we should reflect the character, goodness, and love of God into the world by the way that we live. When God rests on the final day of creation (Genesis 2:2) He is not taking a break because of exhaustion, but rather God has completed the work of creation which He will now oversee, leaving those created in his image to run the day to day operations. Our purpose is to organize the world in such a way that it reflects the purposes and desires of God.

In Genesis the word image is used five different times (Genesis 1:26, 27; 5:3; 9:6). The word image in the Old Testament is usually associated with an object of worship (Exodus 20:4; Leviticus 26:1; Deuteronomy 5:8; 2 Chronicles 33:15). The same word is used of Adam and Eve's

[95] Walton, John H. *The Lost World of Genesis One: Ancient Cosmology and the Origins Debate.* Downers Grove, IL: IVP Academic, 2009, 74.

third son, Seth, who is in the likeness or image of his father Adam. After the murder of Abel by his brother Cain in Genesis 4, God provides another son for Adam. Adam proclaims that "*...God has granted me another child in the place of Abel, since Cain killed him...*" (Genesis 4:25). With the birth of Seth, the line of Adam finally begins to call upon the name of the Lord. Seth marks a turning point for the children of Adam from the murderous Cain, to a son who will honor his parents and God by reflecting the proper image into the world.

Human beings fail miserably in this vocation. If you read through Genesis you are soon confronted with Adam and Eve sinning in the garden (Genesis 3:6), and the first fratricide (Genesis 4:8), and eventually destruction via the flood because of the sinfulness of mankind (Genesis 6:5-7). In only six chapters mankind has managed to mar creation, reflecting an image of greed, pride, and hatred into the world. Human beings are in the image of God, but that image has clearly been marred by sin. This is why in Colossians, Paul refers to Jesus as "*...the image of the invisible God...*" (Colossians 1:15). God wanted his creation to rule and have dominion over all things, mankind failed in the vocation to be the image of God in the world, and so God sent his Son to be the ruler of this world.[96] Jesus is the true image of God reflecting the will and work of God into the world. In Romans, Paul explains it this way: "*For those God foreknew he also predestined to be conformed to the likeness of his Son*" (Romans 8:29). This is the power of an image on full display.

Why does this happen? What causes us to deny our rightful place in the family of God? In part it comes from a denial of how we were created. In Genesis 1 God creates mankind in His image, we literally reflect God into the world, not based on where we were born, our social status, our gender, name, age, or level of faith. Every single person is made in the image of God and reflects that image into the world.

Certainly, we don't always live up to that calling. In Genesis 3 the image of God is cracked, because of our unfaithfulness. But that crack does not mean that the image has been lost, rather it simply means that we are in need of restoration which God one day promises to fulfill.[97]

---

[96] McKnight, Scot. *The King Jesus Gospel: the Original Good News Revisited*. Grand Rapids, MI: Zondervan, 2011.

[97] McKnight, Scot. *Embracing Grace. A Gospel for All of Us*. Brewster MA: Paraclete Press, 2005.

But no matter what we do, we cannot cease to reflect the image of God, because that is how we were made. Richard Rohr puts it this way:

> *"Whatever you call it, the 'image of God' is absolute and unchanging. There is nothing humans can do to increase or decrease it. And it is not ours to decide who has it or does not have it, which has been most of our problem up to now. It is pure and total gift, given equally to all."*[98]

In Matthew 22, Jesus is asked about paying the tax to Caesar he responds in the Socratic method by asking a question in return: "... *Whose portrait [Greek: Eikon] is this? And whose inscription?"* (Matthew 22:20). When Jesus asks whose image is on the coin in Matthew 22:20 the original hearers would immediately recognize that an image conveys a message about a person. Humans are designed to reflect the image of God into the world through their actions (Matthew 5:3-16). The image on the Roman coin was meant to send a message to everyone who used money. In the days before mass media coins were a simple and convenient way to spread a message about who was in charge. When asked whose image is on the coin, the response is simple *"Caesar's, they replied..."* (22:21).

What exactly did Caesar's image on the coin mean, and what was its significance?

There are two groups that confront Jesus in this story, one of them being the Pharisees. The Pharisees lived a life centered on following the Law given through Moses. One of the central commands in the Old Testament is the prohibition of graven images or idols (Exodus 20:4-6). This command was interpreted in a myriad of ways, but during the time of Jesus those who followed the Law felt that false images should be avoided at all costs.

In Matthew 22:19 Jesus asks for a coin. This is significant because apparently Jesus did not possess one of the coins in question; He had to be given one from someone in the accusing crowd. The coin given to Jesus is a denarius, which was a Roman coin that was equal to a working man's daily wage.

---

[98] Rohr, Richard. *The Universal Christ: How a Forgotten Reality can Change Everything We See, Hope For, and Believe.* New York, NY: Convergent, 2019. 61.

> *"The small silver coin was stamped with the head of the Roman emperor and with the letters TICAESARDIVIAVGFAVGVSTVS. The letters represented the Latin phrase, Tiberius Caesar Divi Augususti Filius Augustus, which means Tiberius Caesar, August Son of the Divine Augustus. The words themselves were offensive to Jews. On the back of the coin were engraved a seated female figure and the inscription PONTIF MAXIM, which proclaimed the Caesar to be the sovereign pontiff of Rome's pagan religious system."*[99]

A coin that declared Caesar as the divine son of God and true ruler of the world would have been offensive to any monotheistic Jew. Those who followed the Law of Moses carefully avoided carrying this type of coin in their pocket because by doing so they were literally carrying around a graven image, a violation of one of the Ten Commandments.

Images were a powerful tool in the first century. Any time a person used this type of coin they were in essence cooperating with the claim that the Romans were the rightful rulers, and that the claims of Caesar having divine origins were true. Imagine you were the person handing the coin over to Jesus out of your pocket. With that simple act you have exposed yourself as colluding with the Roman Empire.

In Matthew 21 Jesus drives out the money changers in the Temple. Jesus overturns their tables and chastises them for making the house of God into a den of robbers (21:13). Why were the money changers there in the first place? Because worshippers had to exchange the Roman coins with the blasphemous language of Caesars divinity on them for the Jewish shekel which did not include the image of Caesar.[100]

Now that we understand the power of an image, we need to think through the implication of taxes. The denarius was issued by the Roman Empire to spread the claims of Tiberius, and to also pay the tax back to Rome. Rome issued the coins, and collected the coins back as tribute. In America every four years taxes become a hot button topic. Normally

---

[99] Phillips, John. *Exploring the Gospel of Matthew: An Expository Commentary.* Grand Rapids, MI: Kregel, 2005, 423.

[100] Parini, Jay. *Jesus: the Human Face of God.* Boston: Houghton Mifflin Harcourt, 2013.

the person running for office makes a campaign promise not to raise taxes on average Americans. Even if this is impossible or untrue, the average voter responds to this type of rhetoric, because no one wants to pay a higher tax. In the time of Jesus, taxes were so high on some that it lead to a system of domination where the rich got richer, and the poor were cast aside into poverty and at times even had to sell themselves into indentured servitude to pay off their debts (Luke 16:1-13).

Any would-be Messiah would be asked about the issue of taxes. Many first century Jews reluctantly and bitterly paid the tax, while others revolted. Whenever an uprising took place, the Roman army would mercilessly crush those who resisted their empire, often times crucifying them along the main roads in Israel. These would be revolutionaries were often times left hanging on the cross for days as a sign to anyone else that happened to walk by that dodging the Roman tax would not end well.[101]

If you were a follower of Jesus and someone asked about paying taxes to the evil and blasphemous Roman Empire, you would assume the answer would be a stark rebuke of the evils of the Emperor, and that one day the Messiah would restore Israel to its rightful place of leadership. Less than one hundred years earlier the Romans marched through their country, stole their land, and now they were exacting a harsh tax to be paid back to them as tribute for their protection.

Jesus' response is not what anyone expects. After exposing the Jews in the crowd for participation in blasphemy, He simply responds to the question of if we should or should not pay taxes with "*...Give to Caesar what is Caesar's, and to God what is God's*" (Matthew 22:21). How did the crowd respond? *"When they heard this, they were amazed. So they left him and went away"* (22:22).

Why were the crowds amazed at His response?

First, Jesus directly confronts the entire Roman system and the false claims of Caesar. Jesus is effectively saying "if Caesar wants to make claims of divinity, give him back his worthless coin because true divinity does not look like this." Caesar minted the coin, and in order to pay the tax demanded that the Jews participate in spreading his false claims through their economic activity. Jesus is simply saying that

[101] Wright, N.T. *Matthew for Everyone*. London: SPCK, 2004.

Caesar's claims are fine, but they are not worth the coin that they are printed on, so simply give them back to him. Jesus seems to be saying to pay the tax. At the same time Jesus also seems to be calling for a new revolution.

Jesus is not concerned with the claims of Caesar, because he is operating in a different mode of being. Instead of having to make claims of divinity, and having to back those up with harsh taxes, and military strength Jesus is offering His followers a different path forward. When asked the question of whether or not His followers should pay taxes Jesus brilliant response sounds both like a revolution, "give Caesar back his worthless coin", and a command to pay the tax "*Give to Caesar what is Caesar's*".

Jesus final admonition hints at the true answer to the question he was faced with that day. "*...And to God what is God's*" (22:21). Jesus tells his followers to give Caesar back his coin, because faithful devotion to God means that only the one true God should receive our praise. Caesar may make his claims of divine rule, but in reality God is truly in control of all things. Jesus had previously told His disciples about His upcoming fate (Matthew 16:21). Jesus' life would end much like the revolutionaries that refused to pay the tax, on a cross as a spectacle. The powers of the day would one day take His life as well, but instead of this being an end to His revolution, it was only the beginning.

Caesar declared himself to be Savior of the world, the bringer of peace and safety, and the gift of God to the world. These claims were backed up through the strength of the empire, and in the first century thousands depended on Caesar to fulfill these very promises. During the time of Jesus you were confronted with this reality. Whose side were you on? Caesar wanted to reflect his own image of empire and power into the world, and part of that strategy was the images and inscriptions on his coins. Jesus on the other hand calls his disciples to reflect a radically different image, one that reflects the kingdom of God – one of servant hood.[102]

For disciples in the first century, the image on Caesar's coin represented the reality in which they lived. Your world reflected the policies and programs of Caesar, participating in that world through

---

[102] Camp, Lee C. *Mere Discipleship: Radical Christianity in a Rebellious World*. Grand Rapids, Mich: Brazos Press, 2004, 45.

economic activity was simply a way of life. Jesus, though in His answer to the question that sought to trap him hints at a much different world. A world that no longer reflected the image of Caesar, but instead one where His followers would be Icons [Greek: Eikons] reflecting the image of God.[103] This reflection was man's original purpose in the creation story, and Jesus had come to be the perfect example of how to reflect God into the world. But the question remains, what would that world look like, and what would it mean to reflect the image of God into the world?

Imagine a place where a small group of people reject the power structures of the world, and instead live as if they are animated by a different reality. Caesar wanted to create an empire that reflected his image, and he was quite successful at doing so. Being a Roman citizen came with privileges and standing in society. In Roman society those who reflected Caesar's image were ranked higher than those who did not. If you reflected the image of Caesar you could be the member of important clubs and associations that gave you a higher place in society.[104] Caesar provided safety and security. Caesar made sure everyone was fed and clothed. Caesar made sure society was ordered.

Now imagine a small group of people who decide to live reflecting a different image. This small group could take the propaganda of Rome and turn it on its head. No longer is Caesar, Lord, but rather Jesus is Lord (Acts 4:12, 33). This small group no longer feared the wrath of the empire and depended on them for safety, but instead believed that one day God would restore all things. Caesar ruled with might, but this small group would instead embrace weakness. Anyone who refused to reflect the image of the empire soon found themselves hanging on a Roman cross. This group was so subversive that some of their members resisted to the point of hanging on those crosses.

Could this group succeed? Is it possible to change the world even when you have almost no power? Can you imagine a place where instead of society reflecting the image of the powerful; the world reflected the image of Jesus? What would this look like? What would we even call a group like this?

---

[103] McKnight, 2011.

[104] Meeks, Wayne A. *The Social World of the Apostle Paul.* London: Yale University Press, 1983.

The small group of weak, politically and socially disconnected group of people went on to change the entire world because they reflected the image of Jesus. Not just with their words but through their actions[105]. This small group even began to take on the title of "*ekklesia.*" *Ekklesia* is the Greek word for church, and refers to a small group who gathers together in orders to decide communally how their lives should be ordered.[106] This small group of individuals who decided that reflecting the image of God was more important than reflecting the image of Caesar went on to change the world, but how exactly did they do it?

The book of Acts records the foundation of this early group of radicals who sought a better way forward than the one given by Caesar and his images. According to the empire of Rome the quickest way to success was to trample your opponents, and bring your own version of civilization. Anyone who resisted would be punished severely. Those who followed Jesus' words about images in the first century took a decidedly different stance. Instead of the accumulation of power and wealth they instead shared everything they had with each other (Acts 4:32). Instead of looking out only for themselves, they adhered to a political philosophy that believed that anyone in need should be provided for. To reflect God's true image into their world they were willing to give to others in need, especially when they had more than they required for themselves. This radical type of generosity was only possible because this early group decided that they would reflect something different into the world.

Because they believed in reflecting the image of Jesus instead of the image of Caesar the book of Acts tells us "*There were no needy persons among them. For from time to time those who owned lands or houses sold them, brought the money from the sales and put it at the apostles' feet, and it was distributed to anyone as he had need*" (4:34-35).

We vote for and support political candidates because we want our values reflected in society. We join political parties because we want the values of the party reflected in our country. When we vote we are entrusting that the person we elect will reflect our values. In the first

---

[105] Bell, Rob. *Velvet Elvis: Repainting the Christian Faith.* Grand Rapids, MI: Zondervan, 2005, 163.

[106] Camp, 2004. 106.

century the image of Caesar on coins was a way of showing that Caesar ruled, his values were the right values, and the world was meant to reflect his image.

Now imagine a place where there are no needy among us, where we are willing to give of ourselves for others. The needs of others are met because a small group of people decide they will not reflect the world's values of greed, domination, and power. Imagine if a small group of people began to live so counter to the culture of the day that their generosity meant that there were no needy among them. Single moms had their mortgages covered during times of difficulty. Kids who can't afford new shoes for school in the fall have them provided for them. Those who are grieving are comforted through shared meals. The sick are visited, the homeless cease to exist because programs are sustained to meet their needs, and even those who do not believe in the same God are welcomed into a community of love and acceptance.

That is a world that truly reflects God's image.

Image, a word we often associate with a reflection. We are all reflecting an image, the only question is what image do others see when they look at your life?

TYRANT

"It is better to be Herod's pig than his son"
-Caesar Augustus[107]

"When Herod realized that he had been outwitted by the Magi, he was furious, and he gave orders to kill all the boys in Bethlehem and its vicinity who were two years old and under..."
--Matthew 2:16

THE STORY OF HOW I (JONATHAN) CAME TO BE STRANDED ON A SATURDAY morning started with me trying to impress my boss.

Years ago I had the privilege of working with Miami Youth For Christ, an organization dedicated to reaching young people on high school campuses. Every year the staff and volunteers from Youth For Christ would come together for a Christmas party. That year a generous board member offered to host the party at his home. Since there would be dozens of us at this party we needed to transport tables and chairs from our main office to the house for the Christmas party. At our weekly Friday staff meeting my boss asked if there were volunteers to help transport the tables and chairs to the party. I wanted to impress my boss so I immediately volunteered to help out.

We rented a U-haul truck and loaded all of the tables and chairs, and transported them to the house where the party would take place. That night as the party wound down we loaded the truck back up and took the chairs back to the office.

Only one task remained, and that was returning the U-haul truck that we had rented. I was looking to move up even higher in the hierarchy of volunteers so I told my boss that I would return the truck the next

[107] Josephus, F. (1999). *The New Complete Works of Josephus.* Grand Rapids, MI.: Kregel Publications. 567.

day early in the morning before it was due back, and I would do this all on my own so that none of my other co-workers would have to wake up early the next morning to have the truck back before the 9AM deadline.

The next day my alarm went off, and I jumped in my car on the way to the office to return the truck. As I drove to work, I imagined how grateful my co-workers, and more importantly my boss would be that I had gone the extra mile to return the truck early on a Saturday morning. As I pulled into the parking lot and climbed out of my car, it hit me. Once I drove the truck to the U-haul store, how would I get back? In my attempt to impress my boss I had volunteered to return the truck alone, I had not considered how I would get back to my car after I dropped the truck off.

I thought quickly about calling a co-worker, but soon dismissed that idea. I was on a mission to impress everyone, and couldn't bring myself to admit what a foolish mistake I had made. So Saturday morning at around 7:30AM I drove the three miles to the U-haul truck store, dropped off the truck and the keys and made the long slow shameful walk back to my car.

The next week I told no one of my mistake. My goal was to impress my bosses, and I was not about to show them my foolish error, no matter what.

In the first century in Israel two names dominate our understanding of who was the boss of Israel on behalf of the Roman government during the life of Jesus; Herod and Pilate.

Herod the Great ruled over the area of Israel for thirty-four years. He was able to do so because of his cunning nature and keen political acumen. Herod was able to convince both Octavian (who would later become Caesar Augustus) and Antony to place him as the ruler over the area of Palestine. Octavian and Antony were political rivals, and both had ambitions to ascend to Emperor one day. After a brutal fight at the battle of Actium, Octavian defeated Antony and took the throne as Caesar "Augustus" (a title meaning majestic) in 31 B.C. Herod's ability to convince two Roman rulers, who would eventually battle each other for dominance as the sole ruler of the empire, is in itself quite an accomplishment.

Pilate was a procurator, or government representative, in Palestine from 26-36 A.D. He was appointed by Rome to manage the distant land of Palestine, and is remembered for his cowardly actions during the crucifixion of Jesus (Luke 23:1-25).

The story of Herod and his family is one of intrigue, murder, and violence.

Herod was married to ten different women, which resulted in a life of bitter rivalry and family discord. Herod was a brutal ruler who would not stand for any sort of challenge to his authority. Herod had his wife, Mariamne, put to death in 29 B.C., along with her two sons, Alexander and Aristobulus, who were put to death in 7 B.C. Herod also had his first son, Anitpater, put to death because he was a challenge to the rule of Herod.

Herod is best remembered every Christmas as the tyrant who ordered the murder of all children in Bethlehem under two years of age (Matthew 2:16). In his old age Herod became unhinged. Imagine a brutal dictator willing to murder his family and friends to stay in power, while slowly descending into madness in his advancing age. The slow disintegration of Herod's mind coupled with his brutal rule makes the command to murder the innocent in Bethlehem all the more plausible. Only a monster like Herod would command small children to be ripped from their mother's arms in order that he might cling to power for just a short time longer. Thankfully for those he ruled over, he died in 4 B.C. Upon his death his kingdom was to be split into three parts with Archelaus to rule the area of Judea and Idumaea, Herod Antipas (who shared a name with his father, making him difficult to differentiate) to rule the area of Galilee, and Philip to receive Ituraea and the area of Trachonitis.[108] Like his father, Archelaus was well known to be a brutal ruler. Mary and Joseph fled Herod's decree to murder all the children in Bethlehem by sojourning to Egypt. Upon hearing that Archelaus had ascended to a position of power in the place of his father, they purposely avoided coming back to Judea and made their way to Galilee (Matthew 2:22). Herod had ordered the slaughter of innocent children just a few years earlier, and so Joseph and Mary expect no less from his evil son.

Archelaus finds himself a technical ruler over a large area of land. Upon his father's death, Archelaus hosts a seven day funeral, as was

---

[108] Barabas, S., DeVisser, P., & Tenney, M. C. (1963). *The Zondervan Pictorial Bible Dictionary*. Grand Rapids: Zondervan. 350.

tradition for the deceased. If ever there were a case for not saying anything nice about the deceased at a funeral, this would be it. At the conclusion of the mourning period, Archelaus clothes himself in white and heads up to the Temple mount. Archelaus is acting as the true political and spiritual ruler of Judea. It is there that he is accosted by Jewish multitudes, who hurl accusations and complaints about both his father and his prospective rule over them. Archelaus is infuriated. How dare a group of peasants question his right to rule? He burns with anger, possibly now understanding all the more why his father, whom he hated, was forced to rule with so much violence. But Archelaus cannot act hastily and crush his enemies like his father would have. In order for his reign to be considered legitimate he must first get official approval from Rome, and so Archelaus promises the people that he would not take the position or authority of a king over them until it was approved by the overseers in Rome. A trip to Rome is in order, where he would request an audience with Caesar Augustus who would officially designate him ruler over Judea.

The people bombard him with questions about what type of ruler he would be, and like the average politician, Archelaus makes promises that he has no intention of keeping. He promises to lower taxes and to have mercy on those who are currently languishing in prison as the result of his father's brutal regime. The people are exceedingly distraught with the prospect of Archelaus ruling over them in any capacity, but Archelaus keeps his cool because he knows that he must make it to Rome to have his reign officially endorsed by Caesar if he is to be seen as legitimate. For this reason Archelaus avoids making war with the multitudes because such an action would delay his important departure to Rome.[109]

Despite his empty promises of a generous rule, Archelaus soon finds that the crowds who oppose him will not go away quietly. During the time of Passover, Jerusalem would be crowded with traveling pilgrims, there to celebrate a feast. It was during this period of time when nationalism was at an all-time high. Hopes for a revolution against evil foreign rulers reach its peak because the people are celebrating their ancestors' escape from Egypt's brutal regime. Archelaus sends one of his

[109] Josephus, 1999. 728.

generals to the Temple to try and control the crowds, but they rebuff the efforts of the general by throwing stones at him, and driving Archelaus' ambassadors out of the Temple area. The Jewish crowds refuse to leave the Temple area. Archelaus reverts to an action reminiscent of his father. He sends his well-equipped army to crush the protestors. Bloodshed ensues, and his army slaughters three thousand people that day. Those who were able to escape are sent running for the hills.

Now that those who were causing unrest for Archelaus have been dealt with in a decisive way, he decides to make his way to Rome, though he is not alone. His brother, Herod Antipas, is also making his way to Rome for the same reasons: to ask for official approval from Caesar and to be made ruler. Antipas brings with him witnesses to testify against his brother. Sabinus, Herod Antipas' friend, testifies on behalf of Antipas, and before Caesar Sabinus accuses Archelaus while at the same time commending Antipas, instead, to be named ruler over the Jewish nation.

Archelaus once again must be contemplating his father's methods. Maybe violence and brutality is the only path to success.

Not only does Sabinus stand and accuse Archelaus, but his very own brother, Herod Antipas, then takes center stage and issues a blistering rebuke. Herod Antipas accuses his brother of setting himself up as a king without proper permission from Rome. Before the appearance before Caesar, Archelaus sat on the throne in Judea, even going so far as to wear the royal crown. Anyone who dared to take action like this against Herod the Great would certainly have been met with the death penalty. The funeral he threw for his father? It was merely a show. During the day Archelaus was seen in mourning, but at night he drank excessively showing no remorse for his father. A stupor brought on by alcohol was likely the cause of the slaughter of three thousand innocents, whose bodies were heaped together in the temple in a way that could only be called desecration. In fact, the only reason that Archelaus had even a remote claim to the throne was the result of him taking advantage of his father in his advanced age. Only a deathbed change in the will led to Archelaus being mentioned as a possible successor. Archelaus took advantage of the degeneration of Herod's mind to have him sign a deathbed commission elevating him to ruler in his will.

To add insult to injury, members of Archelaus' own family testify against him, confirming the evil deeds that he had done and the disaster that would certainly result by him being made ruler.

Archelaus at this point must be burning with anger. He has been betrayed by his brother and family. Perhaps this is why Herod the Great was so ruthless in dealing with challenges from within.

Archelaus cannot allow these accusations to go unmet; and so on his behalf, a friend Nicolaus pleads the case for Archelaus. Nicolaus tells Caesar and all those assembled before him that it is not the fault of Archelaus that bloodshed had become so common, but rather it was the result of the enemies of Caesar who had provoked the attack. Archelaus had actually exercised a great amount of self-control in only slaughtering those three thousand in the Temple, and in fact his actions were justified to keep the peace. After the defense of Nicolaus, Archelaus comes before Caesar and, in a show of humility, falls down on his knees bowing before the Emperor of Rome. In this mind of Archelaus, this act of humility was far beneath him, but he swallows his pride and hatred because he knows that he will have his revenge.

The testimony of all interested parties has now been heard, and Caesar is left to make his decision. But before a final verdict is given, one last group is given an audience in front of Caesar. A group of fifty Jews are allowed to speak in the forum before Caesar. They too oppose the rule of Archelaus. They had come to plead for their nation and their well-being, and are supported by eight thousand Jews outside of the council. They level the following accusations against the family of Herod:

> *"He had filled the nation full of poverty, and of the greatest iniquity, instead of that happiness and those laws which they had anciently enjoyed; that, in short, the Jews had borne more calamities from Herod, in a few years, than had their forefathers during all that interval of time that had passed since they had come out of Babylon, and returned home, in the reign of Xerxes."*[110]

The Jews are adamant that they do not want to see Archelaus as their ruler and beg Caesar to hear their cries. At this point after all

[110] Josephus, 1999. 734.

sides have been heard, it is now time for Caesar to make a decision. He dissolves the assembly for a few days to consider all sides and to return a verdict. To the surprise of many, despite the many warnings about the evil of Archelaus, Caesar gives one half of Herod's kingdom to him, with the promise to make Archelaus a king one day if he proves himself worthy of the title. The other half of the kingdom was split between Herod Antipas and Philip. The brutal killings of three thousand people, a pilgrimage to Rome to appeal to Caesar, the testimony of family, friends, and subjects who confirm that Archelaus was not fit to be ruler go unheeded. The Jews now find themselves once again under the ruler of a maniacal tyrant.

Thankfully, Archelaus' rule was short, spanning only ten years. He ruled over the people in a foolish barbaric way (much like his father) and because of this was banished to Gaul in 6 A.D.

Twenty years later, we find another leader making a trip to the capitol city ready to take on the role of ruler. In Luke 19 Jesus tells his followers a parable that begins this way:

> *"He said: "A man of noble birth went to a distant country to have himself appointed king and then to return. So he called ten of his servants and gave them ten minas. 'Put this money to work,' he said, 'until I come back.' "But his subjects hated him and sent a delegation after him to say, 'We don't want this man to be our king.'* (19:12-14).

Jesus tells a parable based on the story of Archelaus, and his trip to Rome to secure what he felt was his right to rule over a portion of Israel. The people are incensed at a ruler, whom they believe to be unworthy of the calling of leadership, and grumble about his leaving on a trip. Knowing that the background to this story is the failed kingdom of Archelaus brings clarity to the people's disgust with the request.[111] When Archelaus made his way to Rome for his hearing before Caesar, he would have appointed servants to watch over the kingdom until his return. Their command was to run the kingdom as if they were

[111] Wright, N. T. *Jesus and the Victory of God*. Minneapolis: Fortress Press, 1996. 632-639.

Archelaus. Imagine being one of the servants in this scenario, working for a king you despise and being told to act on his behalf while he is on a trip in a foreign land seeking not to better the kingdom but to gain greater power for himself. In essence, the Jews are being asked to participate and perpetuate the evil rule of the family of Herod.

Upon his return the master calls the servants before him to inquire about what they have done while the he was away.

> *"He was made king, however, and returned home. Then he sent for the servants to whom he had given the money, in order to find out what they had gained with it. "The first one came and said, 'Sir, your mina has earned ten more.' "'Well done, my good servant!' his master replied. 'Because you have been trustworthy in a very small matter, take charge of ten cities.'*
>
> *"The second came and said, 'Sir, your mina has earned five more.' "His master answered, 'You take charge of five cities.'*
>
> *"Then another servant came and said, 'Sir, here is your mina; I have kept it laid away in a piece of cloth. I was afraid of you, because you are a hard man. You take out what you did not put in and reap what you did not sow.' "His master replied, 'I will judge you by your own words, you wicked servant! You knew, did you, that I am a hard man, taking out what I did not put in, and reaping what I did not sow? Why then didn't you put my money on deposit, so that when I came back, I could have collected it with interest?'*

At this point we begin to see that the master is demanding, and that any failure could be met with serious consequences.

> *"Then he said to those standing by, 'Take his mina away from him and give it to the one who has ten minas.' "'Sir,' they said, 'he already has ten!' "He replied, 'I tell you that to everyone who has, more will be given, but as for the one who has nothing, even what they have will be*

> *taken away. But those enemies of mine who did not want me to be king over them—bring them here and kill them in front of me'"* (Luke 19:15-27).

The end of the parable paints a picture of a ruler who is harsh, judgmental, and even murderous. This type of ruler would have been familiar to the original audience because it was reminiscent of the rule of Herod and his family.

This parable and its parallels (Matthew 25:14-30) have been at times understood apart from both their historical context and the wider Biblical teaching of the return of the King in the person of Jesus. The original audience of this parable would have in the back of their minds two competing narratives: that of Archelaus who travelled to a distant land in order to receive a kingdom, and at the same time the hope that one day a king would come from within Israel to take up rightful ownership of the kingdom and restore the land from exile. In this parable these two narratives collide. The story of Archelaus, and at the same time, the story of Jesus making his way to Jerusalem indicating that he is about to establish a kingdom.

In the first century, the original audience would listen to this parable and sense their deep anguish and hatred towards rulers like Archelaus who had gone off to a foreign land, leaving servants in charge while he masqueraded as a caring ruler before the emperor, only to return and further torment those he did not find productive during his absence. If you were a faithful Israelite, the very act of refusing to expand the kingdom of Archelaus by exempting yourself from participation in his kingdom while he was away could have been seen as the ultimate act of resistance to the evil empire. The startling brutality at the end of the parable where the master has his enemies killed before makes more sense if we realize that the story of Archelaus is the background to this parable. To have those individuals killed before the ruler for their lack of participation is exactly the type of leader Archelaus was. The murder of yet more servants in his kingdom would have surprised no one.

But at the same time, this parable is also about the coming of Jesus as King to Israel. Would Jesus be the same type of ruler? Would those who refused to follow him be treated in the same way? The parable functions both as a rebuke of the vacuous leadership of Archelaus and at the same time contrasts that with the coming of the true King Jesus to Israel. In the same way that Archelaus returned to evaluate the work of his servants, soon the one true God was going to come and evaluate the work of the faithful. This promise of the return of God is made clear through the Old Testament prophets.[112]

> *In that day they will say, "Surely this is our God;*
> *we trusted in him, and he saved us.*
> *This is the Lord, we trusted in him;*
> *let us rejoice and be glad in his salvation"*
> (Isaiah 25:9).

God would one day return to his people and it would be welcomed as a day of salvation.

> *Say to those with fearful hearts,*
> *"Be strong, do not fear;*
> *your God will come,*
> *he will come with vengeance;*
> *with divine retribution*
> *he will come to save you."*
>
> *Then will the eyes of the blind be opened*
> *and the ears of the deaf unstopped.*
> *And those the Lord has rescued will return.*
> *They will enter Zion with singing;*
> *everlasting joy will crown their heads.*
> *Gladness and joy will overtake them,*
> *and sorrow and sighing will flee away*
> (Isaiah 35:4-5, 10).

Salvation is coming. God is coming with vengeance, but only for those who are evil. The righteous members of the family of God long for the coming day when they will be saved.

[112] Wright. 1996. 612-653.

How beautiful on the mountains
are the feet of those who bring good news,
who proclaim peace,
who bring good tidings,
who proclaim salvation,
who say to Zion,
"Your God reigns!"
Listen! Your watchmen lift up their voices;
together they shout for joy.
When the LORD returns to Zion,
they will see it with their own eyes.
Burst into songs of joy together,
you ruins of Jerusalem,
for the LORD has comforted his people,
he has redeemed Jerusalem.
The LORD will lay bare his holy arm
in the sight of all the nations,
and all the ends of the earth will see
the salvation of our God (Isaiah 52:7-10)

In Luke 19 Jesus is on his way to Jerusalem. The Old Testament prophets promised that one day the Lord would come to redeem Jerusalem as He establishes his Kingdom.

All of these verses speak of the glorious return of the King to Zion (Jerusalem). Isaiah dreams of the day that the one true God will come at last to set up the kingdom, restore the fortunes of the faithful, and hold those who are evil accountable. These verses speak of a glorious restoration that is to come, but much like when Archelaus returned from Rome, so too will God return to the land and judge those who have not met the requirement to act in justice, mercy, and love.

But your iniquities have separated
you from your God;
your sins have hidden his face from you,
so that he will not hear.
For your hands are stained with blood,
your fingers with guilt.

Your lips have spoken falsely,
and your tongue mutters wicked things.
No one calls for justice;
no one pleads a case with integrity.
They rely on empty arguments, they utter lies;
they conceive trouble and give birth to evil.

Truth is nowhere to be found,
and whoever shuns evil becomes a prey.

The Lord looked and was displeased
that there was no justice. (Isaiah 59:2-4, 15).

These passages and others like it (Isaiah 66; Ezekiel 43; Zechariah 2, 8; Malachi 3) all speak of the return of God. However, two key distinctions should be made between the two stories. First the return of God is not the return of a distant absentee landlord who has only gone away to pursue selfish ambition.[113] Rather, God would return in the sense that His chosen people would be restored, and all would come to worship the one true God (Psalm 2). The God who cannot be contained in the highest heavens or in a man-made temple would never be considered as "absent" (1 Kings 8:27). Instead, what the people hoped for was a king who would come into his kingdom and establish a reign of justice for all, punishing the wicked and vindicating the righteous. This was exactly the opposite of what Archelaus had done, but it was exactly what Jesus was saying He would do.

At this point those who considered themselves as a part of the chosen nation of Israel might very well rejoice – they were to be exalted, and their evil enemies would be brought to justice.

Those who served in the kingdom of Archelaus would not be surprised to find a king who returned and had all those who did not serve his will slaughtered, but when we read the parable in Luke 19, we should wonder: Is this the way Jesus will treat His servants? Is there no difference between the two kingdoms?

This parable does two things at the same time, first it retells the story

[113] Wright, N. T. *The New Testament and the People of God*. Minneapolis, MN: Fortress Press, 1994. 307-320.

of Archelaus, and second, it warns the people of Israel that the coming of God is imminent. For those who were faithful to the commission of God, this is a day of rejoicing, but for those who have forsaken the ways of God and relied instead on empty ceremony, or had forgotten to live a life of justice and love towards others, the return of God would be a day of refining fire.

> *"Woe to you who long*
> *for the day of the LORD!*
> *Why do you long for the day of the LORD?*
> *That day will be darkness, not light.*
> *It will be as though a man fled from a lion*
> *only to meet a bear,*
> *as though he entered his house*
> *and rested his hand on the wall*
> *only to have a snake bite him.*
> *Will not the day of the LORD be darkness, not light—*
> *pitch-dark, without a ray of brightness?"*
> (Amos 5:18-20)

Those in this passage who are arrogant are warned. If you think you are on the inside, one of the chosen people, beware. If you have come to think of yourself as holy and set apart because of your status, position, race, or empty actions, the day of the Lord will surprise you. The Jews had practiced a set of rituals that they believed set them apart from the outsiders, but what was God's response to these rituals?

> *"'I hate, I despise your religious festivals;*
> *your assemblies are a stench to me.*
> *Even though you bring me burnt offerings and grain offerings,*
> *I will not accept them.*
> *Though you bring choice fellowship offerings,*
> *I will have no regard for them.*
> *Away with the noise of your songs!*
> *I will not listen to the music of your harps.*
> *But let justice roll on like a river,*
> *righteousness like a never-failing stream!'"*
> (Amos 5:21-24)

The return of Archelaus was a day of darkness because it meant that the evil ruler had returned to torment the people with his brutal regime all the more. The return of God in the form of Jesus' life, death, and resurrection would be a regime of justice and righteousness. In Amos 5 the prophet warns the people that their acts of empty worship, days of feasting, their church services and offerings are all empty expressions before God without justice. The people of Israel celebrated complex rituals of sacrifice, holy days, and purification to set themselves apart from other nations. But in the end God declares to them that all of their works are flailing noise because they were performed without justice and mercy.

Those who thought of themselves as insiders will be exposed. In the gospels Jesus' harshest warnings are not for those outside of the faith, but rather the most serious consequences await those who consider themselves to be set apart. It is easy for us today to look at others in judgment, while exalting ourselves as faithful Christians because of our good works. But the prophets warn us, beware of such arrogance. The King is returning, but what the King wants is right living, mercy, generosity, and kindness towards others. If we have spent our time claiming to be part of the family of God, but our actions towards others have not been generous, loving, and kind, we are in danger of harsh punishment.

Luke goes on to give an example of what the type of living that the coming king is looking for. In Luke 21 we find the following story:

> *As Jesus looked up, he saw the rich putting their gifts into the temple treasury. He also saw a poor widow put in two very small copper coins. "Truly I tell you," he said, "this poor widow has put in more than all the others. All these people gave their gifts out of their wealth; but she out of her poverty put in all she had to live on."* (Luke 21:1-4).

In Archelaus' world, the poor widow would have been insignificant, unworthy of even the slightest consideration, but in Jesus' kingdom this widow is whom we should emulate. The King is coming to claim the place on the throne, and if we are not like the widow in our generosity, we are in danger of judgment because we are not being faithful servants while the master is away.

If we claim to love God, but there are those without the proper means to support themselves in our neighborhoods and we turn a blind eye to them, we are not being faithful servants (Micah 3). If we take advantage of others in order to get ahead ourselves, we are not being faithful servants. If we treat people from different backgrounds, nations, or religious affiliations differently because they are not like us, we are not being faithful servants. If we exclude others whom we decide are undesirable or sinners because we worry that they are unredeemable, we are not being faithful servants (Luke 19:1:10). If we consume more and more without thought for how our increased consumption keeps others in a state of need, we are not living as faithful servants (Luke 21:1-3). When we rely on military might to crush our enemies, instead of beating our swords and guns into gardening equipment, we are not living as faithful servants (Micah 4:3).

All of these ideas may not reflect what our society might claim to be the right way to live, but we are not living for our society, our leaders, our political party, or our religious institutions. We are living for the Kingdom established by Jesus.

We have all certainly tried to impress our bosses one way or another. I tried to do so by going the extra mile and returning a truck, but all of us have tried to make ourselves look better through our actions. Unfortunately, sometimes we rely on methods that are antithetical to what Jesus really desires from us as a way to try and impress him.

Tyrant is a word which brings to mind the worst of all people. If we want to be faithful servants, we will live like servants of Jesus and not like servants of a tyrant.

JUDAS

"Your bodies are mortal, and subject to fate; but they receive a sort of immortality, by the remembrance of what actions they have done."[114]
--Josephus

"...Then he went away and hanged himself"
--Matthew 27:5

TWO THOUSAND YEARS AGO A REVOLUTIONARY LEADER CAME ONTO THE scene in ancient Israel. He called disciples who were willing to follow him to their deaths because of his teachings. He taught that piety towards God, and not the size of an army, was the ultimate source of victory over enemies. He cleansed the Temple in Jerusalem, driving out those who had placed false idols there, and rededicated the entire sanctuary to God. As a result of his leadership his followers were able to defeat the enemies of the one true God, and restore true worship to the Temple. This Jewish leader helped to fulfill the prophecies of the Old Testament prophet Daniel by defeating the evil actions of a foreign ruler. He was the leader of the Jewish nation during a time of great conflict, but because of his actions the people who worshiped the one true God were eventually victorious. His exploits were so well known, and his followers so successful that every December people around the world remember his life and work through the celebration of a holiday. Today we remember him because his actions changed the course of history.

In the first century there was another leader who has been described in a gospel as an ideal servant because he would perform the ultimate

[114] Josephus, Flavius. *The New Complete Works of Josephus.* Kregel Publications, 1999. 406.

sacrifice for others. [115] His life had such an impact that today his name is known all over the world. In fact his name is so important that parents will normally refuse to use his name for their children. He occupies such an important place in history that a gospel was named for him, the discovery of which was hailed as one of the most important discoveries in the twentieth century.[116] Today there are some scholars who portray him as the real hero of the gospels, because without him the death and resurrection of Jesus would never have been possible.[117] These men changed the course of history with their actions, and today we still remember them. They were both important figures in history, and ironically they share the same name:

Judas.

When my wife and I (Jonathan) found out we were expecting a child in 2016 we were confronted with one of the most important decisions parents can make for their child, choosing a name. We both knew that this decision was one of the first responsibilities we had as parents, and we understood just how important it was. We faced several challenges in making this decision. First my wife and I decided that we wanted to be surprised by the baby's gender. So until birth, we had no idea what the sex of the baby was, which meant we needed not one, but two names that both agreed on. This process was further complicated because we each had the power of veto over a name that we didn't like, and each of us used that veto liberally. As we came closer and closer to the arrival of our child the pressure slowly built. We were frequently asked by friends and family what the gender of the baby was (we didn't know) and what we planned on naming the baby (another question we had to answer with a shrug). I should take the brunt of the blame for this dilemma because I reveled in suggesting that we bestow a Biblical name on our child, for example the often overlooked name Barabbas. It was not until almost the eighth month of the pregnancy that we finally decided on two separate

---

[115] Gathercole, Simon. "The Gospel of Judas." *The Expository Times* 118, no. 5 (2007): 209-15. Accessed December 20, 2018. doi:10.1177/0014524606075050.

[116] Kasser, Rodolphe, Marvin Meyer, and Gregor Wurst. *The Gospel of Judas*. Washington, D.C.: National Geographic, 2008.

[117] Cahana, Jonathan. "Salvific Dissolution: The Mystery of the Betrayal between the New Testament and the Gospel of Judas." *New Testament Studies* 63, no. 01 (2016): 111-24. doi:10.1017/s0028688516000278.

names, one for a boy and one for a girl. On November 23, 2016 our son William David Pedrone was born at 12:20AM. I jokingly told my wife Karen that coming up with the name of our son was more difficult than the actual labor and delivery, after which I learned that when your wife is in labor she is not likely to find your jokes funny in any way.

For weeks we struggled over names, making list after list. Names were added, and names were vetoed, but one name we never considered for our son: Judas.

The name Judas today is synonymous with someone who is treacherous. I have never in my life met someone who is named Judas. Because of Judas Iscariot's betrayal of Jesus this name has been wiped from the list of prospective baby names. In the first century however, the name Judas was actually quite a popular choice. In the work of the first century historian, Josephus, there are fifteen different references to someone named Judas. In fact one of the brothers of Jesus who wrote one of the New Testament epistles is named Jude, a version of the name Judas (Mark 6:3; Jude 1)[118]

When we think of Judas Iscariot we think of someone who is a betrayer, the unfaithful disciple who betrayed Jesus leading directly to His death on the cross. But before Judas Iscariot there was another Judas who led the nation of Israel in a revolt against the Syrians. His heroic life even earned him the nickname "the hammer" because of his ferocity in battle.

Judas Maccabeaus was one of the five sons of Mattathias born in the second century B.C. Mattathias and his family lived in Israel during the time that the evil Syrian ruler, Antiochus, had plundered the Temple and stopped the native Jewish people from performing sacrifices there. Antiochus was a ruthless ruler; after he ended the practice of sacrifice in the Temple, he stole all of the valuable artifacts. The golden candlesticks, golden altar, and even the veils in the temple were taken because they were made of fine linen.

After Antiochus desecrated the temple he then brought into the holy place an altar on which he sacrificed a pig, a terrible offense to Jews who consider pigs to be unclean. He then commanded that temples and altars

[118] Wright, N. T. *Judas and the Gospel of Jesus: Have We Missed the Truth about Christianity?* Grand Rapids, MI: Baker Books, 2006.

be built across the country, on which swine would be offered every single day. Circumcision for all Jewish boys was outlawed, and anyone found guilty of breaking the law against circumcision were killed, some of the infant boys hung by their necks on a cross. Antiochus' actions were so horrendous that Daniel refers to them as the abomination that causes desolation (Daniel 9:27, Matthew 24:15).

Antiochus sought to radically transform the land of Israel, removing all forms of Judaism and replacing the Jewish religion with a Greek style religion and culture. The persecution in Israel was so bad under Antiochus that the Samaritans who lived in Israel, and thus saw the suffering of the Jews decided to further separate themselves. They sent an ambassador to Antiochus begging him for mercy. They even offered to rename their place of worship "The Temple of Jupiter Hellenius" and offered to adopt the Hellenistic ways of Antiochus so he would look on them with mercy. They were so afraid of this evil ruler they were willing to make whatever accommodation necessary to save themselves from persecution.[119]

It is in this period of persecution that heroes arise. Mattathias was a faithful Jew who was zealous for his country and for the Law of God. Mattathias taught his five sons that it would be better to die for their country than to continue to live under this persecution. Mattathias taught his sons to be zealous for their country, and for the Law of God. One day when Mattathias saw one of his fellow Israelites sacrificing in the manner that Antiochus had commanded, Mattathias, along with his sons, attacked the worshipers violently killing both the worshipers and a general in the army of Antiochus. Mattathias and his sons then destroyed the false idols, and the altar that was used to honor the pagan gods. He called other followers, calling all who were passionate for the laws of God and proper worship, to take up their swords and join a revolutionary fight against the evils of the Syrians.

Mattathias was a great military hero, his fame spread far and wide because of his resistance to the evil Antiochus. Upon his death he appointed his son Judas to be the leader of the revolution. Judas inspired his disciples to continue the fight against evil and oppression. Eventually Judas led a band of warriors to Jerusalem, the holy city, where Antiochus

[119] Josephus, 1999. 404.

had defiled the Temple. Judas finds the Temple in shambles. He orders a new candlestick and altars to be brought into the Temple, which he then purified and restored. This celebration of the restoration of the Temple lasted eight days. So profound was the victory that the Jews decided that every year they should celebrate a festival to remember the mighty works of Judas, and so to this day in the month of December, Jews everywhere celebrate Hanukkah.

The name Judas was quite popular in the first century in part because whenever someone heard the name Judas they were reminded of the great revolution against the evil powers that the entire family of Mattathias had led. It was into this world that a few years later Judas Iscariot was born. The name Judas is actually the Greek form of the name Judah, a tribe of Israel from which both David and Jesus descended (Genesis 49:10).

So it should come as no surprise that in the Gospels one of Jesus' twelve disciples shares the same name. Judas the disciple is referred to in the gospels as Judas Iscariot in order to differentiate him from the other Judases of the time. There has been much speculation as to what the name Iscariot means, some have suggested it could mean "assassin", but most likely it was simply a reference to the town that he was from.[120]

Throughout history Judas Iscariot is known as a turncoat and a betrayer, his name brings to mind one of the worst instances of human betrayal in history. In 2006 interest in Judas was revived with the publication of a short gospel that had recently been discovered. The gospel of Judas is part of a codex (an early version of a book) that contains several other letters and epistles. The discovery of this short gospel was not a total surprise, because the church father Iranaeus, Bishop of Lyons made reference to the gospel of Judas in his writings in the second century. The Gospel of Judas is considered to be a gnostic gospel (more on that in a moment). These gospels tend to turn the heroes of the Gospel stories into villains and the villains in the stories into heroes. They subvert our previous understanding, and in some ways they contradict what is considered orthodox understanding of the life and times of Jesus.

The Gospel of Judas is quite different from the four canonical

[120] Gathercole, 2007.

Gospels. In this story, Judas is not the villain who betrays Jesus; rather Judas is cast as the hero. He is the one true disciple that is able to understand the purpose of Jesus life on earth, and his eventual destiny. The Gospel of Judas is considered a gnostic gospel. The word *gnosis* in Greek means knowledge, and normally refers to a special spiritual truth (Colossians 2:3).[121] Gnosticism was a growing belief system in the first century that was grounded in dualism. In this split worldview, the present physical world that we live in is evil, debased, and wicked. Human beings as physical creatures are corrupted. If our physical bodies are corrupted, this means that the creator of our bodies is also corrupt. Our only hope out of this existence is to transcend our human physical existence into a purely spiritual one. This salvation is available to those with the correct *gnosis* (knowledge) that can only be revealed to us by someone from beyond the realm. This secret knowledge would enable someone to escape the physical world and achieve a purely spiritual existence. Simply put, Gnosticism is a denial of the goodness of the creation (and creator) and an exalting of the spiritual world. In the first century, Gnosticism was considered a false teaching, but slowly over time it has crept its way back into some theological systems that teach that our ultimate goal in the future is to escape to the physical world where we will exist in a disembodied state in heaven.

Anyone familiar with the Gospel stories should immediately recognize that these Gnostic Gospels are certainly not in harmony with the four accepted Gospels of the Bible. In Gnosticism, the resurrection of Jesus is denied, because the physical is part of the evil material world, and so the resurrection of Jesus would be considered a failure to transcend the physical because in resurrection Jesus remains in the physical world.

It is within this world of Gnostic thought that the Gospel of Judas comes to us. Some believed that it would change everything about how we read the Bible, because there was suddenly a new gospel that would give us the real story of Jesus unencumbered by two thousand years of church dogma and tradition. In the Gospel of Judas the hero of the story is Judas Iscariot. Judas serves an important purpose, to turn Jesus

[121] Vine, W. E. *Vines Expository Dictionary of Old & New Testament Words.* Nashville, TN: T. Nelson Publishers, 2003.

over to the authorities to be killed because Judas has received the special *gnosis*. Judas knows that the only way for Jesus to truly be the promised King is for him to shed his physical body and achieve a purely heavenly existence. In the gospel Jesus says to Judas "But you will exceed all of them, for you will sacrifice the man that clothes me."[122] Jesus is asking Judas to betray him to the authorities so he will be killed and released from his evil material body. If Judas is faithful to this calling he will enable others to see that the true goal of life is to leave the physical behind and step into the infinite spiritual world where the true God dwells.

The Gospel of Judas teaches us that what Judas did in the garden was not a betrayal; it only appeared that way to those who did not have the proper gnosis. Instead, what Judas did was open the doorway for Jesus to transcend this physical world and join the spiritual world.

The purpose of the Gospel of Judas is to reform the way we view Judas Iscariot. In a way, the purpose is to reclaim his name and legacy which was according to this new Gospel to be soiled by the traditional stories that cast Judas as the ultimate betrayer. The question is, was it successful?

At one point in Israel, Judas was a common name, a reminder to the people of the works of Judas the hammer, the great warrior who cleansed the Temple and restored proper worship. Just a few years later Judas Iscariot changed the perception of the name rendering it obsolete in years to come. But what do the Gospel writers and more importantly, Jesus, tell us about Judas Iscariot?

Whenever the Gospel writers list the names of the disciples they are careful to place Judas Iscariot at the end of the list of disciples (Matthew 10:2-4; Mark 3:13-19; Acts 1:13-19). In Luke 6 the names of the disciples are listed, with Judas occupying the very last spot in the list. Luke adds "*...Judas Iscariot, who became a traitor*" (6:16). John gives us insight into the character of Judas. At a dinner in Jesus honor Mary took an expensive jar of perfume and poured it on Jesus feet. Judas is incensed at this show of honor. He claims that the money from the perfume could have been used to help the poor, but John tells us "*He did not say this*

[122] Wright, 2006. 55.

because he cared about the poor but because he was a thief; as keeper of the money bag, he used to help himself to what was put into it" (John 12:6).

The authors of the gospels were clear in their writings about the character of Judas; he was a traitor and thief, not worthy to be counted among the twelve. But in the gospel of Mark we find Jesus, as He normally does, surprising us with his treatment of the traitor.

As the book of Mark progresses we see clear glimpses that before His death Jesus knew of His ultimate fate. In Mark 8:31, 9:31, 10:45 the author indicates to us that Jesus knows He is headed towards his death and that he purposely sets off towards Jerusalem knowing what awaits Him there. He will be betrayed, and suffer at the hands of the Roman Empire, enduring a most gruesome death on the cross. In Matthew 26 during the last supper between Jesus and his disciples he identifies Judas as the person who would betray him (26:23-25). Jesus even directly confirms to Judas that yes, he is the one who will betray Him.

Jesus seems to know what awaits Him, betrayal by one of his closest companions, which would lead to execution. Jesus even prays that God would be able to take this cup of suffering from him (Matthew 26:42). Despite knowing all of this, Jesus takes no action to stop Judas. If we knew that one of our closest friends was about to betray us, how would we react? If we knew in advance of the betrayal to come, would we try to get them before they got us? Would we seek out some way to harm them in advance so that we would be spared their betrayal?

It is interesting to see that even despite all of this; Jesus seems to hold out hope for Judas. In Matthew 26:50 when Judas comes into the garden to betray him Jesus still refers to him as "friend". In Mark 14 Judas is still referred to as one of the twelve (14:10-11). Even at the moment of the betrayal Judas refers to Jesus as "*Rabbi*" which connotes closeness and even still a friendship between the two (14:45). In all of this Jesus never tells His disciples who was coming to betray Him even though they were more worried that He was speaking directly about them identifying one of them as a turncoat (John 13:22-25). Jesus could have pointed out Judas specifically as the betrayer, and had His disciples on watch for when the moment of treachery would come. He could have commanded his disciples to take Judas into custody so that he could not perform this evil deed. But instead, Jesus waits, calmly, patiently going about his business even though He knows that soon Judas would do the unthinkable. Why does Jesus do this? Why would Jesus not be proactive in His actions to stop Judas?

Both Matthew and Luke tell us the story of Judas' death, each giving different accounts of how Judas died. In Matthew 27 we learn that after the betrayal Judas is filled with grief, and tries to return the 30 pieces of silver he was paid to betray Jesus to the chief priests. His remorse grows so great that after he returns his bribe he hangs himself, ending his own life in a suicide. The money that he returned was used to buy a field to be used as a graveyard which is named a "field of blood" in Matthew 27:8. In the book of Acts Luke gives a particularly graphic retelling of the death of Judas. "*With the reward he got for his wickedness, Judas bought a field; there he fell headlong, his body burst open and all his intestines spilled out*" (Acts 1:18). In the Biblical narrative Judas' death evolves from a simple suicide by hanging to having his guts spill out of his body. This graphic scene was meant to reinforce the idea that in death Judas received his just reward for his betrayal. Both gospel writers make a special point to refer to the tragic end of Judas' life.

Why would they spend precious time and space on the death of a traitor?

After the arrest of Jesus in the garden, because of Judas' betrayal the disciples are conspicuously absent from the last moments of Jesus' life until his resurrection three days after his death and burial. In fact, upon His arrest the disciples flee for fear of their lives (Mark 14:50). The only disciple that plays a role in the trial, sentence, and death of Jesus is Peter, who while Jesus is on trial betrays Jesus much like Judas had done. Three times Peter is asked if he knows Jesus, and three times he denies knowledge of Jesus, even going to the extreme of calling down curses as he swears to his interrogators that he has no relationship with Jesus (Mark 14:71). We now have two traitors amongst the twelve, both Judas and Peter.

In the last moments of Jesus life we are given the story of two disciples, and both betrayed Jesus when he was the most vulnerable.

Imagine the depth of despair Peter must have felt when the rooster crowed, fulfilling the prediction Jesus had made just a few hours prior to His betrayal. When Peter hears the rooster crow, he immediately breaks down and weeps because he knows the depth of his betrayal. Peter was in the garden just a few hours earlier and witnessed first-hand

Judas' treacherous kiss. In fact he even tried to defend Jesus unsheathing a sword and cutting off a man's ear (John 18:10). When Peter saw the depth of Judas' betrayal he was incensed and was ready to fight. But when faced with the very real prospect of death Peter wilts under pressure and becomes a Judas.

Peter is not alone in his denial, the rest of the disciples are nowhere to be found in the last hours in the life of Jesus. Those who had followed Him for three years suddenly abandon Him in the moment of trial. If the story ended here the disciples would be remembered as weak and unworthy. But the story does not end here, even though death is coming quickly for Jesus, resurrection is also on the horizon. Unlike a purely spiritual existence, Jesus will physically, bodily rise from the dead in direct contrast to the teachings of the Gnostics. This resurrection means not only the defeat of death, but also restoration for each of the disciples. Because of this restoration they are remembered not for their moment of weakness, but rather as powerful men who will go on to establish the church of Jesus Christ that still exists to this day.

In Mark's resurrection story three women trudge to the tomb of Jesus to anoint the body of Jesus. They are met at the tomb by an angel who pronounces to them that Jesus is no longer in the tomb for He has risen! Their instructions are to "*...go tell his disciples and Peter*" (Mark 16:7). Why among all the disciples is Peter mentioned? Because Jesus knew about the betrayal, and there was still time for Him to be restored. Jesus didn't give up on Peter.

Because Peter was restored in relationship with Jesus his name is remembered and passed down. Large portions of Christians in the world look to Peter as the first leader of the church, as a person of great esteem. His tomb can be found in Vatican City, one of the most visited places in the world. Peter is remembered as a hero of the faith.

Today, expecting parents may name their children Peter, but they almost certainly will not consider naming their child Judas. Unlike Peter, Judas' relationship is not restored, he takes his own life, and his death is recorded in graphic terms to further disgrace the name of the deceiver. The Gospel of Judas goes to great lengths to attempt to restore the name and character of Judas in vain. While the Gnostic Gospel of Judas provides insight into basic dualistic worldview of the Gnostics, it is not accepted as a true gospel because of its deeply sub-biblical view of the created world. Judas' name goes down in history as someone who committed one of the worst crimes in history.

Why did the Gospel writers refer to only these two disciples after the arrest of Jesus? To show that even though both had betrayed Christ, they both had a chance at restoration. The sad end to Judas' life was self-inflicted, not the result of Jesus turning His back on His close friend. "Indeed, had Judas not killed himself or died suddenly, we may imagine that even the betrayer would have been restored to the relationship and community."[123]

Judas the hammer is remembered for his zeal for God and his fight against the evil empire of the day. Judas Iscariot is remembered as a traitor, who effectively ruined the name Judas for all future generations. What can we learn from the life of Judas? First, that for Jesus no one is excluded from the possibility of restoration. Even those who have directly denied Him have a chance of redemption if they are willing to accept the abundant love that Jesus offers. Second, how will our names be remembered? Will we leave a legacy that will be remembered and will our names be passed on?

When my son was born, my wife and I gave him the middle name David, because my middle name is David. He carries part of my name into the world, and my prayer for him is that he will bring honor to that name. When I am gone from this world, my name will live on through him.

Two men named Judas. The life of one is celebrated every year during Hanukkah; the other is reviled because of his evil deeds. Two disciples play an important role in the final hours of Jesus' life. Both betray him, casting aside three years of friendship, teaching, and living together. In a way, we have all played the role of Peter and Judas. We have turned our backs on Jesus at various moments in our lives, and like Peter and Judas we have a chance at restoration despite our betrayal. Judas rejected that opportunity, ending his own life, and with that act he fully closed himself off to the forgiveness that Jesus offers.

Peter betrayed Christ almost immediately after Judas. His name could be remembered with contempt, but Peter recognized that Jesus

---

[123] Borg, Marcus J., and John Dominic Crossan. *The Last Week: What the Gospels Really Teach about Jesus Final Days in Jerusalem*. New York: HarperOne, 2007. 126.

never turns his back on anyone. With Jesus there is always another chance; restoration and forgiveness are one step away, even for those who have committed the ultimate betrayal. The story of these two disciples challenges us to consider two words and two names: are we a Judas, or a Peter?

Take a moment and consider your own name. How will you be remembered?

LEFT-BEHIND

"A man and wife asleep in bed
She hears a noise and turns her head he's gone,

I wish we'd all been ready

Two men walking up a hill
One disappears and ones left standing still

I wish we'd all been ready

There's no time to change your mind
The son has come and you've been left behind"[124]

--Larry Norman

"Two men will be in the field; one will be taken and the other left."
--Matthew 24:40

Judgment day was coming for me, and there was nothing I could do to avoid it. When you are in Junior high school, your life is measured in days, because you are not old enough to have a long term perspective. This meant that I knew the precise moment that my life would be over; in fact I could count down the hours until justice was served on me. My only hope was for some sort of respite, a miracle from on high that would save me from certain doom. I needed a miracle from God, and that is exactly what I got.

[124] "Larry Norman – I Wish We'd All Been Ready." Genius. January 01, 1969. Accessed February 24, 2019. https://genius.com/Larry-norman-i-wish-wed-all-been-ready-lyrics.

It began on a Friday afternoon at 2:45PM. For a 12 year old boy in school this is the best moment of the week, just a few short minutes of the final bell ringing, and an entire weekend of freedom to play with friends. This moment was made even sweeter because for my friends and I the week ended with P.E., which meant that our final class of the week would be spent playing basketball in the gym. My small group of friends had retreated to the far corner of the gym. We wanted to be as far away from the entrance as possible because we knew what was coming. If we could only just avoid the principal for a few more minutes the weekend would be upon us, and maybe, just maybe there was a possibility that he would forget about us. As a group we were all nervous because we had committed some infraction that week at school, and we were told by our teacher that she would be referring the matter to the principal to determine our punishment. Today I can't remember exactly what we did, but I can clearly remember the dread I felt waiting for that call to come. We did our best that day to avoid the hallways, mostly because the door to the principal's office was located right next to our lockers.

So it was that we found ourselves in the gym on a Friday afternoon trying to avoid all adult supervision. We knew that judgment day was coming, but we hoped by some miracle that if we could make it to the final bell the weekend would wash away our transgressions and we would be saved. With only ten minutes to go in the school day the gym door opened and the principal strode in. He immediately saw us across the gym and pointed directly at our group. Our only hope was miracle, and for some reason God decided to give us a brief respite. We were told by the principal to be in his office first thing Monday morning. Due to the lateness of the day, we had escaped punishment for an entire weekend. We decided this would be the best weekend of our lives because it would likely be our last. I can still remember going to bed Sunday night knowing that when I woke up the meeting with the principal would be the first thing on the agenda for Monday morning. I woke with a pit in my stomach and proceeded to go about my morning routine to get ready for school. As I walked to the window to take a look outside I was greeted with another miracle from God. Snow! Beautiful, wonderful white redemption direct from the heavens. There was so much snow that the roads were covered and school would be cancelled for the day.

God had given me grace that I did not deserve, an entire extra day off school, one more day of life before judgment day would come. I had an entire 24 hours left to enjoy, and with that extra day the hope that after a weekend, followed by a snow day that the principal would have forgotten about us. Certainly when we returned to school on Tuesday we would be spared. Tuesday morning I met up with my group of friends outside in the hallway, all of us were relieved that we had one more day of freedom, and we all hoped that we would be spared. We made it all the way through most of our first hour class before we heard on the school's P.A. system those dreaded words. Our names called off in a list, followed by "to the principal's office please." Judgment day had come.

To this day when someone mentions judgment day my mind wanders to the infractions that I have most recently committed. In the gospel of Matthew Jesus gives one of His longer sermons. In this sermon He warns his disciples that the day of God's return will come quickly without warning (Matthew 24:27). Those who are wise should be ready for His return (24:44, 46). As a child growing up in Sunday school every so often I would hear a message about Matthew 24 about the danger of being "left behind" based on Jesus warning in Matthew 24:39-41: *"That is how it will be at the coming of the Son of Man. Two men will be in the field; one will be taken and the other left. Two women will be grinding with a hand mill; one will be taken and the other left."*

To be left behind was the greatest tragedy that could befall a person. In fact, there is an entire series of bestselling fictional books named after this particular passage. Above all I was taught that I should do everything I could to avoid being left behind, lest I be unprepared for the coming Day of Judgment. There would be no snow day to avoid that punishment. But what if everything I learned about this passage was wrong? What if it would be better for me to be left behind? In order to understand what this passage means we need to look at three distinct themes in the passage. They are: judgment, flood, and the Romans love of a particular athletic shoe.

The first step is to rethink our understanding of judgment, especially in the way that Jesus uses the term. Judgment is what happens in a court room, where a judge who is assumed to be wise and honest declares guilt or innocence. When we think of a judge we often times only consider the guilty, who are there to receive recompense for their actions, but what of the innocent? For the innocent, for the righteous, judgment day is something we long for. The day when we will finally be vindicated because we are not guilty of whatever crime we have been accused of. For the innocent person, judgment day is something to long for, because when a wrong has been done, all the innocent want is their day in court to be vindicated.

> *"The word judgment carries negative overtones for a good many people in our liberal and post-liberal world. We need to remind ourselves that throughout the Bible, not least in the Psalms, God's coming judgment is a good thing, something to be celebrated, long for, yearned over. It causes people to shout for joy and the trees of the field to clap their hands. In a world of systemic injustice, bullying, violence, arrogance, and oppression, the thought that there might come a day when the wicked are firmly put in their place and the poor and weak are given their due is the best news there can* be."[125]

For Israel, judgment day was longed for because it was the day at long last that God would bring justice to the world. Those who had remained faithful to God would be vindicated, the evil doers would be put on trial, and their deeds would be exposed for the entire world to see. Those who had suffered in silence remaining faithful would be exalted; those who denied the truth and goodness of God would be dealt with in a climactic way. Psalm 98 reaches a crescendo when it proclaims that all those who are righteous should look forward to judgment day. *"Let the rivers clap their hands, let the mountains sing together for joy; let them sing before the LORD, for he comes to judge the earth. He will judge the world in righteousness and the peoples with equity."* In John 5 Jesus tells his followers that judgment is coming, but those who have followed the ways of Jesus have crossed from death to life. Judgment is simply the process of purifying our lives in order to prepare us for that life to come.

Judgment is also a serious matter. Throughout the gospels judgment

[125] Wright, N. T. *Surprised by Hope: Rethinking Heaven, the Resurrection, and the Mission of the Church*. New York: HarperOne, 2008. 137.

is portrayed with stark violent images, not because God is a violent God, but rather to underscore the weight and seriousness of the judgment to come. Judgment is a sober activity, but it is decidedly not the means that God uses to destroy a person. Our desire for our enemies to enter into judgment simply reveals our fallen nature and perhaps our own need for purification. Paul elaborates on the purpose of judgment in 1 Corinthians 3: 13-15. "*Their work will be shown for what it is, because the Day will bring it to light. It will be revealed with fire, and the fire will test the quality of each person's work. If what has been built survives, the builder will receive a reward. If it is burned up, the builder will suffer loss but yet will be saved—even though only as one escaping through the flames.*" If we were to honestly assess our actions we would find there are times when we are righteous, and there may be more times when we are not. We are neither fully righteous nor fully depraved, our actions vacillate. At times we live up to our calling; at others our actions are quite frankly embarrassing. In 1 Corinthians 3, the judgment is a purifying judgment meant to burn away all the dross of our lives, leaving us with what is pure. For some this process will be more painful than for others because of the lack of good works in their lives, but for all the judgment is a process of purification, a process that heals our broken nature. "Perhaps judgment is a process rather than a verdict. Perhaps its fire is the cleansing fire that burns away the dross of our lives; its sufferings and the consequence of the knife wielded by the divine Surgeon who wounds to heal."[126]

The second important aspect of this passage is Matthew's reference to the flood in 24:37 "*As it was in the days of Noah, so it will be at the coming of the Son of Man.*" The flood story is found in Genesis 6-8, and is one of the most familiar stories of the Old Testament. Noah is commanded to build an ark because soon God will flood the entire earth. Noah is faithful to God, and when the flood waters come, Noah and his entire family is saved while all of those not on the ark perish. "*The waters rose and covered the mountains to a depth of more than twenty feet. Every living thing that moved on the earth perished – birds, livestock, wild animals, all the creatures that swarm over the earth, and*

[126] Polkinghorne, J. C. *The God of Hope and the End of the World*. New Haven: Yale University Press, 2002. 130.

all mankind" (Genesis 7:20-21). Everyone in the ark was saved, but those who were not were taken away into judgment.

In the flood those taken were swept away in the flood, those who were left behind survived in the ark. When Jesus begins this portion of the sermon with a reference to Noah he is warning his hearers that to be taken away is to be taken in judgment, to be left behind is to be considered among the righteous who will be saved.[127] This is further emphasized in Luke's version of this sermon. Luke records his version of this sermon in chapter 17. The disciples ask Jesus "where Lord?" in reference to where those who are taken end up. His response: "… *Where there is a dead body, there the vultures will gather"* (17:37). This is clearly a reference to judgment, and something that everyone should seek to avoid.[128]

First century Israel was dominated by the Romans. The Roman Empire was vast, powerful, and excelled at proclaiming their dominance through various methods of propaganda including coins, buildings, and memorials.[129] The Romans were powerful and they celebrated that power frequently. If you lived in the first century one word that would come to mind when you thought of the Empire was victory, because the Romans were almost always victorious. The Roman goddess of victory was *Nike* in Greek, from which the popular shoe and athletic apparel brand, is named. If they existed at the time, every Roman soldier would have been outfitted in the latest Nike brand shoes, because Romans loved to celebrate the fact that they were always victorious over their enemies.

> *"Victory personified was emblazoned everywhere in the Roman Empire. Soldiers carried images of Victory into battle on their flags and trophies. Senators burned incense to Victory as they entered the Roman senate building. Cities erected statues of Victory or Nike with her foot*

---

[127] Wright, Nicholas Thomas. *Matthew for Everyone.* Louisville, KY: Westminster John Knox Press, 2004. 127.

[128] Middleton, J. Richard. *A New Heaven and a New Earth: Reclaiming Biblical Eschatology.* Grand Rapids: Baker Academic, 2014. 225.

[129] Crossan, John Dominic. *The Historical Jesus: The Life of a Mediterranean Jewish Peasant.* San Francisco: HarperSanFrancisco, 1992. See especially chapter 2.

> *on the globe, symbolizing Rome's conquest of the whole world. Coins portrayed her standing beside the emperor, reminding anyone who handled money of Rome's military success.*"[130]

One particular example of the Romans use of Nike to proclaim their dominance over everyone else in the world can be found on the Arch of Titus which was erected in 81 A.D. Titus was born in 39 A.D. and was the son of the emperor Vespasian.[131] Titus was the commander of the Roman army in 70 A.D. when the Romans put down a revolt by the Jews, eventually decimating Jerusalem, and destroying the Temple. Despite ruling for only two years over the Roman Empire an arch was erected in his honor in the year of his death celebrating the destruction of Jerusalem and the Temple. Jesus' sermon in Matthew 24 is the result of the disciples asking him about the destruction of the Temple, which Jesus predicted (Matthew 23:37-38; 24:1-2).

The Arch of Titus celebrated this very event. On one side of the arch, scenes of conquest are carved, including a menorah captured from the Temple. The Roman soldiers are portrayed as taking away the captives from the war into captivity. Titus rides in a chariot driven by the Roman goddess, while the god Nike crowns his head with a wreath symbolizing his victory of the enemies. On the arch was the inscription *"The Senate and the people of Rome, to Divus Titus, son of the divine Vespasian, Vespasian Augustus"*. The inner archway portrays Titus being carried to the heavens by an eagle. This process of divination was known as an apotheosis; it represented the elevation of an individual to a divine status.

Anyone who saw this arch would immediately understand who the powerful were. This arch was a reminder to everyone that when Rome came to town to conquer, being taken away meant a life of subjugation and slavery. To be one of the fortunate who were left behind was indeed a blessing.

These three themes, judgment, flood, and Nike inform how we

---

[130] Rossing, Barbara R. *The Rapture Exposed: The Message of Hope in the Book of Revelation*. Basic Books, 2007. 105.

[131] Barabas, S., P DeVisser, and Merrill C. Tenney. *The Zondervan Pictorial Bible Dictionary*. Grand Rapids: Zondervan, 1963.

should understand this passage. To be left behind is desirable; to be taken away is to be taken in judgment. So how should we respond?

Matthew tells us that the return of God will come quickly, and so we should be prepared. *"Therefore keep watch, because you do not know on what day your Lord will come"* (24:42). The coming of the Lord should not be an event that we dread; quite the opposite. The coming of God and judgment should be longed for by the faithful, because it is in that day that God will finally redeem all things through purification. Our good deeds will be shown in the light of day, evil will be exposed. For those living in the way of Jesus, this is our final vindication. We should then live in a way that anticipates this future coming of God. We should be vigilant in good deeds, and be a faithful steward of all that God has given us (24:46-47).

Judgment day is a day we look forward to because it means that the righteous judge will pronounce our work in this world to be fruitful. The small things we did in life will finally come to light. The kind word we spoke to a person in need, the anonymous gift we gave because we have more than we need, the time we donated a coat for those in the cold, and the invitation that was proffered to someone who would have instead eaten alone (Matthew 25:31-40). These works of righteousness which were hidden from the spotlight will finally get the attention they deserve because judgment day is the day we have been waiting for. To be taken away leads to disaster, to be left behind means salvation from the enemy.

So the next time someone mentions the words judgment day to you, you can assure them that you are eagerly anticipating that day. If someone warns you about being left behind, you can smile, knowing that to be left behind is to avoid the conquest of the enemy.

Judgment day is coming, and you won't need a snow day to save you.

TETELESTAI

"Finishing a job means the job is done"[132]

"It is finished"
--John 19:30

IT WAS A HAPPY DAY. MY WIFE AND I (DINO) WENT TO OUR CREDIT UNION to make the arrangements to pay off our thirty year mortgage. As a result of saving and sacrifice we had paid the loan off in less than 20 years. In order to purchase a home there was no other way for us to have enough to pay up front. So we borrowed the money. Now we were finished. I remember going into the bank office and chatting with a bank official.

"There is still some costs related to paying this off." Her words went through me like a knife.

"Costs? I thought we paid it off"! It wasn't that we did not have the funds to pay more. It's just that I wanted this finished.

The word finished is interesting. Synonyms include ruined, doomed, beaten, and threatened. The word also means to end or complete an action. Finished may speak of the end of a romantic relationship which is sad, or the paying off of a mortgage which produces a pleasant reaction.

Tetelestai is the Greek word that refers to our English word 'finish'. The verb *teleo* means to complete or accomplish something. Several years ago I watched my son, Adam, come across the finish line of the Philadelphia marathon. Quietly I said to myself *tetelestai*. He did it. He finished it. My son told me that was one of his goals. He wanted to finish the Philadelphia marathon. He did what he said he would do.

When Jesus hung on the cross He said *tetelestai*. He was not just saying 'this is over' or 'I survived this.' He was saying I did what I said I

[132] "Job." Dictionary.com. Accessed February 23, 2019. https://www.dictionary.com/browse/job.

would do. The Greek word is actually in the perfect tense which means, 'This took place and it is true today and, in fact, is in effect today. This word is the shout of victory. This word speaks to the accomplishment of a worthy goal. It reminds us that the goal is completed.

Although I will have future expenses like taxes, repairs, and maintenance of the house there is no longer a mortgage. It is done.

When Jesus, the Savior of the world, made this proclamation from the cross He was addressing several truths.

The first truth is that the innocent died for the guilty. As Jesus went through His trial that is recorded in the gospel accounts it becomes obvious that the charges against Him were fictitious. The rulers of the Jews claimed He made Himself to be God. The passages in Scripture where Jesus performed actions on the Sabbath (Matthew 3:11; 12:10; Mark 3:1-6; Luke 13:10-17, 14:5; John 7:23, 9:16) were actions that put Him in the place of God. When Jesus faced the Sanhedrin there were a variety of charges that did not stick against Him.

> *"The chief priests and the whole Sanhedrin were looking for evidence against Jesus so that they could put him to death, but they did not find any. Many testified falsely against him, but their statements did not agree. Then some stood up and gave this false testimony against him: 'We heard him say, 'I will destroy this temple made with human hands and in three days will build another, not made with hands.' Yet even then their testimony did not agree. Then the high priest stood up before them and asked Jesus, 'Are you not going to answer? What is this testimony that these men are bringing against you?' But Jesus remained silent and gave no answer. Again the high priest asked him, 'Are you the Messiah, the Son of the Blessed One? "I am,' said Jesus. 'And you will see the Son of Man sitting at the right hand of the Mighty One and coming on the clouds of heaven.' The high priest tore his clothes. 'Why do we need any more witnesses?' he asked. 'You have heard the blasphemy. What do you think?' They all condemned him as worthy of death."* (Mark 14:55-64)

The Jewish charge was blasphemy. The rulers of the Jews were under Roman authority. As Pilate tried the case he came to the conclusion that there is no fault in Jesus. Pilate's goal was to come to a compromise. Yet there was room for concern in the Roman world. Jesus was drawing large crowds, many believed in His teaching. He looked like the Messiah to many. If the Jewish leaders could somehow paint Jesus as a rebel to Rome it would help their cause.

Jesus, however, clearly told the people to "*...give to Caesar what is Caesar's.*" (Matthew 22:21; Mark 12:17; Luke 20:25) Although Jesus claimed to be the Messiah, He clearly spoke out as having no desire to fight against the Romans. "*Jesus said, "My kingdom is not of this world. If it were, my servants would fight to prevent my arrest by the Jewish leaders. But now my kingdom is from another place*" (John 18:36).

The charge against Jesus that stuck was blasphemy. The Jews wanted to kill Jesus because He claimed to be God (John 5:18; 10:30).

Tetelestai occurs twice in Scripture, in John 19:28 (where the word means accomplished) and as we have seen in John 19:30 where Jesus completes his purpose and work. The innocent one - Jesus - died for the ungodly - all humanity.

What was it exactly that Jesus finished? What was his goal? What does the 'it' refer to? What was finished? To begin with Jesus fulfilled the law. In Matthew Jesus explains to his disciples: "*Do not think that I have come to abolish the Law or the Prophets, I have not come to abolish them but to fulfill them*" (Matthew 5:17). The New Testament book of Galatians clearly teaches "*...the law was put in charge to lead us to Christ that we might be justified by faith. Now that faith has come, we are no longer under the supervision of the law*" (Galatians 3:24-25). The 'it' refers to the law. Jesus fulfills the law.

Jesus is the long-awaited Messiah. His message is clear. The only way to God the Father is through the Son. 'It' refers to Him being the long awaited Messiah. The disciples may not have expected the Messiah to die on the cross, the victim of the Roman system of imperialism, but in Jesus death he actually achieves a great victory over sin and death. We are either with Jesus or against Him.

Jesus, therefore, is God in human flesh. The incarnation tells us that God became a man. This God/man came to save people. "*Jesus answered, I am the way and the truth and the life. No one comes to the Father except through me"* (John 14:6). The 'it' refers to the fact that God intervened into the world of human history and gave His life for lost sinners.

Jesus came to reconcile people back to Him. The word reconciliation refers to a restoration. The synonym refers to bringing back together a reunion. How does someone come back to God? We come to Him because He made us in His image. We are separated from Him because of sin. He restores us to fellowship with God through the work He accomplished at the cross.

'It' also refers to the work of mercy that God has provided. Mercy is compassion given when it is not deserved. Jesus had the power to come down from the cross and punish all those who were cheering the gruesome act against God the Son. Instead He offers mercy. Grace is undeserved favor. Mercy is withholding what someone deserves.

'It' refers to the purifying of the bride of Christ. Lost sinners through Jesus stand before the Father as if they had never committed one sin.

'It' means that Jesus fulfilled the law, He is the long-awaited Messiah, He is God in human flesh, He has reconciled people to Himself, provided mercy, and given God the glory by purifying and bringing to the Father a pure bride.

What is the meaning of 'is'? Most dictionaries state that 'is' refers to the third person singular present of *"to be"*. This word is used to identify a person, event, or thing. *Tetelestai* is teaching us that nothing more needs to be added. God will add no more. God the Father in heaven declares righteous all those who come to Jesus by faith for their salvation. The work of redemption is done.

I recently wrote a book called 'The Beginning.' It is the story of early Christianity. In the first chapter the first sentence the book commences with, "The work of Jesus Christ was finished. He died, was buried, rose again. A key Biblical term is redemption. Redemption means 'to buy back'. In Christian theology the word (Greek *apolutrosis*) speaks of the deliverance from our sins. The word in the Old Testament Scripture refers to a metaphor of releasing or setting free from bondage. There must be a payment."[133]

---

[133] Pedrone, Dino, The Beginning, WestBow a division of Thomas Nelson, 2019 pg.1

Bible teacher Warrren Wiersbe writes, "When an artist completes a picture, or writes a manuscript, he or she might say, 'It is finished'. The death of Jesus on the cross completes the picture that God has been painting, that He has been writing for centuries."[134]

The eternal debt was paid for sin, and humanity now has the privilege to please God through the death of Jesus Christ. Any religion or man-made system to find God is insufficient. Jesus said, 'It is finished.' He really means it.

When I left the credit union, I was reminded that there were actually a few other small fees that I had to pay. The team at the credit union was very kind, and made me aware that I had overlooked some small matters. That's the way life is. It's hard to really finish some things, however, I can tell you the mortgage is paid off.

The word *tetelestai* means that Jesus has finished all that He came to accomplish. The next time you finish something you can think of this word, and how Jesus used this word at the end of his earthly ministry.

I still have some expenses. Taxes, upkeep, maintenance, repairs and it goes on and on. It is a great feeling to have no mortgage. When it comes to our salvation the judge of the universe has declared that what Jesus did at the cross is enough. Nothing needs to be added and nothing to be subtracted. It is done.

---

[134] Wiersbe, Warren, The Bible Exposition Commentary. Cook Publishers 2001 pg. 384

MESSY

"The command 'be ye perfect' is not idealistic gas. Nor is it a command to do the impossible. He is going to make us into creatures that can obey that command"[135]
--C.S. Lewis

"Taking Jesus body, the two of them wrapped it, with the spices, in strips of linen..."
--John 19:40

RECENTLY MY (DINO) WIFE WAS ILL, AND IT FELL TO ME TO DO THE MANY tasks around the house that were usually hers. One of the assignments was to make supper. My father was a professional chef and my siblings all had remarkable cuisine abilities. Even my children seem to know their way around the kitchen. I, however, have neither such gift nor calling. Since I was the only one at home, I undertook with great enthusiasm the task. Her request was very simple, scrambled eggs and bacon plus an order of toast.

My first assignment was to locate the eggs, bacon, toast, toaster, and other ingredients. It was rather remarkable to recognize my lack of familiarity with the kitchen. My wife, Bobbi, is an outstanding cook and her desire is to be in control of the kitchen, and I am very much in favor of this idea!

I set out to make the simple meal and after several requests to my wife on the location of items, we were both surprised that the food was edible. As I was patting myself on the proverbial back, I did begin to recognize that this assignment must have been one of the simpler dinner requests. I assumed that is why she made the request and that perhaps her palate didn't desire just consuming scrambled eggs and bacon, but one that I would be able to prepare.

---

[135] Lewis, C. S.. *Mere Christianity*. New York: Walker &, 1987. 160.

Then I heard a friendly voice, "don't forget to clean up!" Frankly it never dawned on me there was more to this meal than the preparation. Although I have jumped into the middle of cleanup after most meals, few of them were from my preparations. As I left our cozy family room that we call the 'Gathering Room' and entered our kitchen, I saw a small but challenging disaster in front of me. There were egg shells, cartons, a glob of butter, frying pans, dishes, cups, glasses, some grease on the stove, excess bacon, and what appeared like numerous other small items I did not even remember using. The cleanup of all the mess began.

Since I did not think through the results of what the meal would look like, I ended up taking much more time than an experienced person would need. There was one word for this part of the process – messy!

Life is full of complex situations. Life can be confusing and at times extremely difficult. For no apparent reason, confusion and disorder just happen. On other occasions we have caused the mess or perhaps someone else is the culprit. Life can be, at times, messy.

When Jesus Christ died on the cross, He hung there for about six hours. Crucifixion was one of the methods used by the Roman Empire to carry out capital punishment for those who were guilty of criminal crimes. It was reserved for the insurrectionists, vilest of criminals, slaves, plus foreigners. The Jewish religious leaders accused Jesus of proclaiming Himself to be the king. The Jewish method of insurrection was stoning. For the Romans crucifixion was also used as a deterrent against future issues with capital crimes.

The crucifixion is now over. Jesus is dead. The messy work of taking Him off the cross is next. Who will take the body of Jesus away? "*Later, Joseph of Arimathea asked Pilate for the body of Jesus. Now Joseph was a disciple of Jesus, but secretly because he feared the Jews. With Pilate's permission, he came and took the body*" (John 19:38). This wealthy secretive follower of Jesus desires the body of the Lord for burial. He is from Arimathea, a town that has little documentation. It was a town of Judea (Luke 23:51). "The little town is identified with Ramleh where David came to Samuel (1 Samuel 19)".[136] Although there is wide speculation and various ideas about this man, little is known about him.

[136] Lionel Smithett Lewis "St. Joseph of Arimathea". Glastonburg Vicar. All about God copyright 2002-2018) Question; Who was Joseph of Arimathea?

What we do know is that he was an important man, mentioned in all four gospels (Matthew 26:57-60; Mark 15:43-46; Luke 23: 50-55; John 19:38-42).

He was a member of the Sanhedrin. His wealth was commonly accepted and evidenced by the fact that he owned this valuable tomb that Jesus was placed in. Mark explains that he is well respected, and Luke indicates he is not consenting to the decision to crucify Jesus.

In the apocryphal book of Peter, Joseph appears as a friend of both Jesus and Peter. However, this author is far more comfortable following the teaching of the scriptures on him. The fact is, he is very important in the burial of Jesus, although little is known of him.

Joseph receives help from another member of the Sanhedrin, Nicodemus. Nicodemus first appears in scripture to have a conversation with Jesus about His teachings and apparent recognition that Jesus, at least, is a rabbi sent from God. Nicodemus is captivated by the knowledge of Jesus but also the works of Jesus fascinates him. He proclaims to Jesus,

> *"Rabbi, we know you are a teacher who has come from God. For no one could perform the miraculous signs you are doing if God were not with him"* (John 3:2).

The lengthy conversation of a person's need to be born again is clearly defined by Jesus, that He alone is the entrance into God's kingdom. Nicodemus is next mentioned in John 7:50, 51 where he reminds the Sanhedrin the law instructs that a person should be heard before judgment or condemnation. Jesus and His teachings were making many uncomfortable and there were those who wanted to make quick work of disposing of this future king. Nicodemus was having none of this encroachment on the rabbi.

Nicodemus then appears to help Joseph after the crucifixion to provide the embalming spices for the preparation of Jesus in his burial. Both Joseph and Nicodemus are there at His burial. For Jewish people, in the days that Jesus lived, the burial of the dead was very serious business. No dead body should be left unburied. It was considered the right for all Jewish deceased to have a decent burial. During the time of Christ when a person died, their eyes were to be closed and the body was to be washed. This was customary and taken from Old Testament documents. (Genesis 50:1). The body was anointed with perfumes. "Nard was the most usual of these, but myrrh and aloes were used."[137] The body was also wrapped in a shroud and a special cloth (napkin) around the face. The hands and feet had cloth around them. Due to the climate, burial was usually immediately within eight hours after death. Friends would go to the home to grieve with the family and to pay their respects. Some professional mourners were hired and there would be a procession with the family and friends taking turns carrying the body. A large round stone would be rolled at the opening of the tomb. The mourning would last for up to 30 days for the closest of the family members. After a year or more the family would return to gather the bones of the deceased and place them in an ossuary.

Jesus had some faithful followers. There was Peter, John, James, Matthew, Andrew, and others. Where were they? Taking someone down from the cross and following through, even for the worst of criminals was to be practiced, but those closest to the Lord are not to be found. This was messy business, blood; the stench of death, the disappointment of following a false Messiah had overwhelmed those closest to Jesus. But here are Nicodemus and Joseph. Those disciples who were not there would come forth later after the resurrection. It is interesting to note this. The family of our Lord did not go back to get the bones after one year. No bones were available for the ossuary. Why? Jesus rose again. At the time of the crucifixion event, however, very few joined in this messy business.

It seems to me that we often shy away from messy business. It is more convenient to look the other way. Frankly, that is what the early apostles did. They decided that they were in a dilemma and this Jesus they had been following may not be what they thought. However, just out of humanitarian kindness, it would seem they should have been there for Jesus in His last hours. The fact is clear that it is tough to be around when things are getting messy.

In July 2003 several things happened to me that produced a huge

[137] Pope, Charles. "What Were the Rituals Associated with Death and Burial in Jesus' Day?" Community in Mission. May 28, 2015. Accessed April 05, 2019. http://blog.adw.org/2014/08/what-were-the-rituals-associated-with-death-and-burial-in-jesus-day/.

mess. My only brother died in a fire. My daughter was married. My daughter's new grandfather died in an accident. A dear friend's wife died in an airplane crash and my wife was going through major cancer surgery. This all happened in a little over one week.

These types of events become rather messy. Emotional, spiritual, physical, and social challenges were abundant. The church I pastored at the time was amazing in their care for our family. I remember two events that helped me to learn to become involved in the mess of another's life.

The morning my wife was going to surgery I watched the gurney take her away. I felt very alone as I walked toward the cafeteria to get a coffee and relax, when I noticed someone standing in a doorway that looked familiar. It was my friend, Rudy Holland. Rudy and I have been friends for years. My wife met him when he was speaking at a conference and came home to tell me how outstanding his message was. Shortly thereafter I met him and that commenced a wonderful friendship. I said, "Rudy, what are you doing here?" I lived in South Florida and he lived in North Carolina at the time. He flew in early that morning. "I came here to be with you." was his reply. "If you want a coffee, I will buy you a coffee. If you want breakfast, I'll buy that. If you want a sandwich, you got it. If you want a steak I'll buy that."

"Now you're talking!" I joked.

You see Rudy understood what to do as a friend when life seems like such a mess. Years before this Rudy and his lovely wife, Doris, had a son. His name was Paul and he was destined to follow the steps of his father as a preacher. Paul had a very serious disease and over a long period of time Rudy and his wife watched Paul slowly slip into eternity. During many of the challenging days a mutual friend of Rudy's and mine would come to the bedside of Paul and sit with them, Harold Wilmington. Harold wrote many best- selling Bible handbooks but I remember him best for sitting there when my buddy was going through a messy time. Now Rudy sat with me through my messy time.

A few days later I was home with my wife during her convalescence and the doorbell rang. All the way from Tennessee were Jerry and Marie Traister. Jerry was the best man in my wedding, and I was the best man in his wedding. There they were during a messy time of our lives.

When I talk about messy, I mean those chaotic times that occur in our lives. We can't enter into all of them with everyone but there are some people that will need us, and we are the Joseph of Arimathea or Nicodemus that will make a difference for them. Life is messy. Someone needs to help with the clean-up. Sometimes it is a listening ear, other times it is paying someone's mortgage.

The nice thing about helping to clean up the mess is that it makes things better for everyone involved.

ARRIVAL

"He who loves the coming of the Lord is not he who affirms that it is far off, nor is it he who says it is near, but rather he who, whether it be far off or near, awaits it with sincere faith, steadfast hope, and fervent love."[138]
--Augustine

"…So we will be with the Lord forever."
--I Thessalonians 4:17

We all look forward to an arrival. Whether it is the airline landing to bring you to someone you love or your first year college student arriving home for the holidays, there is something special about an arrival.

As I (Dino) pen these words my wife and I are waiting for a friend from college to visit us. We both married classmates from the college that we attended together over 50 years ago. My wife and I are looking forward to seeing her. Her husband recently passed away, and so now she frequently travels alone. Life can bring such quick changes that we are unprepared for.

As we were waiting we received a text that her car broke down and it will be 6 hours before she can arrive. Although it is repaired and ready to go it is still a long time. My wife and I will take her to dinner and enjoy time with her. Waiting for someone we want to see makes me anxious.

When I travel to see my grandchildren it is always delightful to see them anxiously waiting for grandpa and grandma to arrive. We shower them with love because it is such a blessing to see them. We are all so busy that when these moments of blessing arrive we want them to linger.

[138] "Augustine of Hippo Quotes (Author of Confessions) (page 7 of 29)." Goodreads. Accessed February 24, 2019. https://www.goodreads.com/author/quotes/6819578.Augustine_of_Hippo?page=7.

The last words of Jesus remind us of His arrival. They are recorded in the next to last verse in Revelation. Here Jesus said "*Yes, I am coming soon*" (Revelation 22:20). Three times in this chapter Jesus has proclaimed that He is coming again. "*Behold I am coming soon* (Revelation 22:7). "*And behold I am coming soon...*" (Revelation 22:12).

The word "behold" is a term that is used to grab attention. In all three verses we are told that Jesus will come quickly. Many interpret this to mean soon. A better understanding is that when Jesus comes He will come unexpectedly. We should regard the coming of Christ as imminent. The imminent return of Christ means that there are no signs necessary to be fulfilled until Jesus comes again. The Father knows the timetable. "*No one knows about that day or hour, not even the angels in heaven, nor the Son, but only the Father*" (Matthew 24:36).

The first time Jesus came He went to the cross, died, and was buried, then rose again from the grave for our salvation. (1 Corinthians 15:1-6). The second time He will come to reign and to rule. The return of the Lord is a constant theme of the New Testament. All nine of the New Testament writers mention the return of the Lord. "It is alluded to more than 300 times in the New Testament"[139]

The Bible is so very clear on Jesus' return. There are a myriad of ideas on how this will happen. I have my ideas and positions theologically on the Lord's return. Like most of us, I think I am right. However, I would venture to say that it is far more important to learn that when Jesus is talking about His return that He is looking for obedience.

Bible scholar Eugene Peterson said it so well..."Obedience is the thing, living in active response to the Living God. The most important question we can ask a text is not, 'What does this mean?' But 'what can I obey?' A simple act of obedience will open up our lives to this text far more quickly than any number of Bible studies and dictionaries and concordances."[140]

As followers of Jesus Christ we should remember that we are accountable to be stewards of the time, money, and talents that God has given us. If, however, you have not yet accepted Jesus Christ as your

---

[139] Thiessen, Henry Clarence. *Lectures in Systematic Theology*. Grand Rapids, MI: Eerdmans, 2001. 442.

[140] Peterson, Eugene H. *Eat This Book: A Conversation in the Art of Spiritual Reading*. Grand Rapids, MI: William B. Eerdmans Publishing Company, 2006. 71.

Savior I would strongly recommend for you to recognize your need. The Bible teaches that we are sinners and that we can do nothing to save ourselves.

Jesus Christ is God in the flesh. He died to take away your sins and rose again to give you new life in Him, and to prepare you to live your life for Him that will proceed into eternity with Him forever. Trust Him today. There is no miraculous prayer that saves you but you can pray something like this. "I come to you Jesus and realize you died for me. Thank you for paying the penalty for my sins. I here and now accept you into my life as my Savior. I give myself to you." I recommend that you find a good church that believes in the Bible and attend faithfully to grow your faith.

So here I sit. We are waiting for our friend. I am sure she will arrive soon. We will have a good time together. She will then leave and we will not see each other again for a period of time. In a few weeks I go to see my grandchildren. I cannot wait to arrive and to be with them.

Coming and going with people who are important to us leaves us a little empty. But one day Jesus will come and we will eternally be with Jesus. Now that is something to look forward to! I am in the ranks of those looking for the arrival.

The next time you anticipate an arrival, think about how we all long for the return of the King.

GPS

"Scripture, however, possesses a unique spiritual value and capacity to change lives."[141]
--Richard Schultz

"He leads me..."
--Psalm 23:2

Recently I (Dino) spoke in a Bible conference in upstate New York. My wife was feeling under the weather so I traveled to my destination and spent two days speaking at the conference. I told my wife that I would leave quickly after the last service to come home. The trip was a couple of hours from home and there were three turns to get me on my way. I certainly wouldn't need my GPS to make three simple terms.

I made the appropriate turns and was on my way. My thoughts were on how well the conference went, my wife's health, and the upcoming week. I decided to turn on the radio and found a station with some pleasant music. After driving for an hour I decided to stop and get a cup of coffee as my eyes were becoming heavy. Caffeine does a number on me and brings me to a new sense of awareness, so I decided to check my phone for the emails that had been causing my phone to ring constantly. I sipped my coffee and answered a couple of emails. Then I decided to call my wife. I checked my GPS to let her know the time of my arrival. At first glance I assumed there was something wrong with the GPS. I was not one hour from home but nearly three hours away. How could this be? I had 3 turns only to make. Then it hit me like a ton of bricks. Instead of heading south I was heading north. No wonder I did not recognize some of the small towns I was traveling through. I needed

[141] Schultz, Richard L. *Out of Context: How to Avoid Misinterpreting the Bible.* Grand Rapids, MI: Baker Books, 2012. 28.

someone to blame. I could not have made such a foolish mistake. It must have been the faulty GPS. But then I realized I never checked it.

Then I thought about the three different people who gave me directions about how to get home. Each of them told me the exact same thing, were they all wrong? Finally I came to my senses and realized that I made one wrong turn and now was paying the penalty. I called my wife and tried to think of how I could play the victim. Her sweet response was a gentle reminder that this is not the first time this had occurred. This was a different trip but I have found myself in similar circumstances. So now I made a two-hour trip much longer because I did not check the directions.

Sometimes our life is like this. There are plenty of Bible characters with similar stories.

One of my favorite Bible characters is the apostle Peter. In my commentary on Peter I wrote the following:

> *The life of Peter is a familiar story. Either we have been where he has been in our spiritual walk or someone close to us has had a similar experience. Peter was amazed about the Rabbi who had selected him. The Rabbi was Messiah. The elation the Apostle Peter experienced is found in many of the accounts of his conversations with Jesus. But then he fell. He fell big time. He denied the One he claimed was Messiah. Was his life over? If Jesus was the Messiah, would he have another chance?*[142]

John 21 provides rich insight into Peter's comeback. This chapter contains an account of one of the resurrection appearances of Jesus Christ. This is the third time Jesus had appeared to his disciples as a group.

The disciples had fished all night, and caught nothing. Jesus asks them to throw their net on the right side of the boat; the result was a miraculous catch of 153 fish! To say the least Peter is impressed. Very quickly he swims to Jesus. The disciples are now back with their Lord.

After a delicious breakfast served by the Lord there is a conversation

---

[142] Pedrone, Dino. *The Influence of Peter.* XULON Press, 2012.

that Jesus and Peter have about feeding sheep. The sheep will ultimately be the many people Peter will reach. Jesus tells Peter that he has a primary role in the development of the Christian faith. The conversation begins..."Simon...Do you love me" (John 21:15). Three times the Lord asked Peter the same question.

The first time Jesus asks the question he uses the Greek term *agapos* meaning "Do you love me dearly?" Peter's response is a lesser form of the word. It is the Greek term *phileo* meaning to treat affectionately, to befriend, or to approve of (21:15). Jesus tells him that he will have the opportunity to teach, exhort, advise, or speak to the Lord's sheep.

In the second question Jesus uses the same term and Peter responds again with the lesser term. On the third question Jesus uses the same term that Peter had been using *(phileo)*. Jesus lessens the term and asks Peter as he has been responding, "Simon son of John, do you love me?" (21:17). Peter responds in like manner using the Greek word *phileo*. Peter is teaching us a great lesson here in human behavior.

Previously the disciples had journeyed with Jesus and arrived at a place called Caesarea Phillipi. Today that area is called Banias. It is a beautiful spot with a cool body of water. When Jesus predicted His death, burial, and resurrection it was Peter who reprimanded the Savior. In Matthew 16 we have the record in verses 13-23. Jesus asked His disciples, *"When Jesus came to the region of Caesarea Philippi, he asked his disciples, "Who do people say the Son of Man is?" They replied, "Some say John the Baptist; others say Elijah; and still others, Jeremiah or one of the prophets. "But what about you?" he asked. "Who do you say I am?" Simon Peter answered, "You are the Messiah, the Son of the living God."* Jesus highly acclaimed the accuracy of Peter's answer. Later on after this event As Jesus predicted His passion Peter could not grasp such an idea and took the Lord aside and rebuked Him. *"God forbid it Lord. That shall never happen to you."* Jesus rapid, direct response was powerful. *"Get behind me, Satan! You are a stumbling block to me; you do not have in mind the things of God, but the things of men"* (Matthew 16:23). The Lords words of caution to Peter were not heeded. Peter told Jesus he would fight for Him and he proved his point when he cut of the ear of the guard Malchus when the soldiers came to the garden of Gethsemane (Matthew 26:51). Peter thought he was right. He was not, however, following the words of instruction from the Lord.

Then the terrible heartache came! He denied the Lord three times! As Jesus is heading to the crucifixion Peter lies three times and denies his Lord. The rooster crowed. It is at that moment an event takes place that this author senses would stay with Peter forever. It is recorded one time in Scripture. *"the Lord turned and looked straight at Peter ..."* (Luke 22:61). Here is a highly decorated apostle who has miserably failed. It appears his ministry is over. He probably would never forget that look. Perhaps the nights prior to the resurrection he would close his eyes in sleep only to see His Savior's look. He will be a name either lost in infamy or one viewed as a miserable failure for running at the worst moment. His integrity and standing were forfeited. Three times he denies his Lord at the worst possible moment.

A short time later after his denial we find Jesus reunited with Peter at breakfast. Three times He asks Peter if he loves him. The same number of times Peter denied the Lord. Peter cannot use the stronger word because he doesn't trust himself. He uses the lesser word. It is here that Jesus shows His love. The last time Jesus Himself uses the lesser word. He uses *phileo.* He comes down to Peter's level. Just as the Savior came to this sin cursed earth and stooped to become a man so He stoops to Peter's level.

Peter shows wisdom here. The man who bragged about how he would never let his Lord down has realized that bravado had no place in the kingdom. We who follow Christ realize He is Lord and we are simply servants.

Jesus finishes His teaching with Peter with familiar words ..."*Follow Me*" (John 21:19). At the beginning of the Lord's ministry Jesus original call to the disciples was the same message ..."*Follow Me*" (John 1:43).

What does it mean to follow Jesus? The Greek rendering is to follow one who precedes and joins Him as an attendant. It means to be an apostle and side with his party. The obvious question then is this: How do we know what He wants from our lives? The answer is that He has given us a book that details to us about being a disciple. There are many things in our lives we will not grasp nor understand. We will, however, have direction on how to be a follower of Christ and then one day spend eternity with Him. That book is the Bible. It is the guidebook; if I had to describe the Bible in a word it would be our GPS system.

This week I head out to another trip. This one is to Israel. I have a driver taking me to an airport I seldom fly from. There are a number of confusing roads. One thing is for sure. I will make sure I have my GPS with me to check his.

Following directions is better than taking extra time and wasting the most valuable commodity we have, time. If we are willing to follow the teachings of Jesus in scripture it will save us.

NAPKIN

"Easter means that the powers of this world do not have the last word. To use the ancient Latin phrase, Easter is about Christus Victor – God in Christ triumphed over the powers that enslave and afflict the whole of creation."[143]
--Marcus Borg

"Who is it you are looking for?"
--John 20:15

"OH DEAR, I THINK I'M BECOMING A GOD."[144]

These are the supposed last words of the emperor Vespasian. He is said to have uttered these words on his deathbed. A person's last words are often remembered, sometimes profound, and at times strange.[145] What inspired Vespasias dying words? It all started with Julius Caesar.

Julius Caesar was the Roman Emperor from 49-44 BC. He ascended to this title through a series of impressive military victories, establishing himself as the sole ruler of the Roman Empire. Because the military victories of Caesar were swift and decisive, he was named dictator of Rome. Caesar would rule the Roman Empire until the Ides of March (March 15, 44 BC) when he was ambushed and stabbed to death in the Roman Senate. In his will, Caesar named Octavian to be his sole heir.

Octavian, better known by the later adopted title of Caesar Augustus, was the grandnephew of Julius Caesar, and after a brutal war with Mark Antony (who also claimed a right to be leader of Rome)

---

[143] Borg, Marcus J. *Jesus: Uncovering the Life, Teachings, and Relevance of a Religious Revolutionary*. San Francisco: Harper San Francisco, 2006. 290.

[144] Wright, N.T. *The Resurrection of the Son of God*. Minneapolis: Fortress Press, 2003, 55.

[145] Socrates last words as reported by Plato were "*Crito, we owe a cock to Asclepius. Please, don't forget to pay the debt.*" "Socrates." Ancient Greece. Accessed March 17, 2019. http://www.ancientgreece.com/s/People/Socrates/.

ascended to the position that Caesar had occupied. Octavian ruled as Roman Emperor from 27 B.C. – 14 A.D. After the death of Julius Caesar a rumor spread through the empire that witnesses saw a comet streak through the night sky which was interpreted to be the soul of Julius ascending to the gods. This rumor was meant to bolster the claim of Octavian to the throne because Octavian then could claim the title "son of divine Caesar" because he was the successor to Julius Caesar.

One of the ways that Octavian spread this propaganda was through coinage. In the ancient world coins were the chief medium of mass communication, and Octavian had coins minted with his picture and the title "son of divine Caesar" engraved on them.[146] This practice of promoting a Caesar into divine status became common after the time of Octavian. After the death of an emperor, the Roman propaganda machine spread word that the departed leader had ascended to the heavens to live on forever. This practice of divinization was passed down to subsequent emperors and other important figures as an honor upon their death. As Vespasian nears death, his fear of becoming a god is due to the fact that he knew those who survived him would elevate him to the position of god upon his death.

This process of divinization sometimes led to fear among the citizens of Rome. Nero was emperor of Rome until his death in 68 AD. He was known as a particularly brutal emperor, and his death was the cause of rejoicing for many that he persecuted while alive. However, soon after his death stories began to spread amongst some of his soldiers that he had either not died, or that he would somehow make a triumphant return from the dead.[147] These stories struck fear into the hearts of individuals within the Roman Empire. They had finally been freed from the evil Nero, and now rumors of his return would send many into periods of mourning. In 422 A.D. Augustine wrote that many Christians of his day believed that Nero was the antichrist that Paul wrote about in 2 Thessalonians 2.[148] In Revelation 13 the apostle John writes about a beast with ten horns and seven heads that comes out of the sea (13:1). The beast is said to have a seemingly fatal wound, but

---

[146] Wright, 2003. 56.

[147] Ibid., 68.

[148] Augustine *City of God*. Accessed March 17, 2019. http://www.ccel.org/ccel/schaff/npnf102.iv.XX.19.html

somehow the wound is healed, allowing the beast to continue his rule of destruction over the people of God, some of which are deceived into following this evil ruler (13:3-5). In the ancient world popular rulers who died in an unexpected manner were believed not to be dead, but rather in hiding, waiting for a climactic moment where they would return and reclaim their throne. Many followers of Nero believed after news of his death that he was not truly dead, but rather in hiding waiting for this moment.[149]

John gives a further description of this beast in 13:18, where he describes the name of the beast as equaling the numerical value of 666. If the Greek name "Neron Kaisar" is transliterated into Hebrew the numerical value of the title of Nero is equivalent to 666.[150] Citizens in the Roman Empire in the first century were quite fearful of the return of the monstrous rule of Nero.

Stories of rulers becoming gods may sound silly to modern readers. We do not fear the return of evil rulers after their death. We are confident that when dictators are brought to justice in our world no manner of intervention could bring them back. In the age of enlightened thinking we no longer believe that upon a person's death that they ascend to heaven via a comet. However, if you have ever visited Washington DC you have likely seen the Americanized version of this myth.

The United States Capitol building in Washington DC was first completed in 1800. Over the period of the next fifty years, legislators soon realized as the United States grew in size and more and more representatives were elected from newly formed states, that the capitol building was quickly being outgrown. That led to an expansion of the Capitol building, which in turn led to the decision to replace the old dome that dominated the center of the building with a new dome that would act as the centerpiece. Most visitors to Washington DC take time to visit this historic building. One of the highlights is the capitol rotunda, a circular room that lies directly beneath the massive dome.

The Capitol rotunda is one of the most breathtaking places

[149] Crossan, John Dominic. *How to Read the Bible and Still Be a Christian: Struggling with Divine Violence from Genesis to Revelation*. New York: Harper One, 2016. 182-185.

[150] Perriman, Andrew. *The Coming of the Son of Man, New Testament Eschatology for an Emerging Church*. Milton Keynes, U.K.: Paternoster, 2005. 215.

in Washington DC. The walls are lined with massive portraits commemorating important events in American history. But if you were to gaze up 180 feet into the air you would see the underside of the massive dome, and one of the most peculiar works of art in the nation's capital building. The "Apotheosis of George Washington" was completed by Constantino Brumidi in 1865 and represents one of the first attempts in US history to deify an American President. Much like Caesar thousands of years ago, George Washington is represented in this frieze as ascending on the clouds into the heavens becoming a god. Washington sits on the clouds in the middle of the painting surrounded by thirteen maidens representing the thirteen original colonies of the United States. Washington is clothed in royal purple as he looks down over the country that he helped create. On the very edges of the circular dome are scenes dedicated to war, science, marine life, commerce, mechanics, and agriculture. At the center of all of this sits Washington. The word apotheosis in the title of the work is a reference to the idea that this art depicts George Washington ascending to the heavens just like Caesar to become a god.

Caesar, Octavian, Vespasian, and George Washington; all important men from history, all said in some way to have ascended to the heavens to become gods. While each of these men will go down in history, what is interesting is that none of them are actually worshipped today. If on a Sunday you wished to attend the church of Vespasian you would be hard pressed to find a local congregation dedicated to the memory of the Emperor. Each of these men were said to ascend to the heavens, a truly impressive feat. But that falls far short of what the gospels all say happened to Jesus upon his death. The difference between Jesus and these men of history is a simple word: resurrection.

This book is comprised of a series of words from the life of Jesus that have changed history, none of these words is more important than this final one: resurrection.

We wrote this book as a father and son, two people on the journey of faith who have been changed by the words of Jesus. We end this book with the story of resurrection and what it means to each of us.

For me (Jonathan) resurrection means the renewal of all things.

Jesus lived in a world where souls were said to have ascended to the heavens to live on forever, but in the ancient world they recognized the difference between a disembodied soul and resurrection. A soul ascending into heaven was certainly possible (and hardly provable), but no one would have claimed that after death that one of the Emperors actually came back in physical form. When the gospels tell us that Jesus had risen from the dead they were speaking of something that had no parallel in ancient world.[151] Resurrection is not resuscitation, resurrection is not a soul escaping the earthly confines to a pure experience in heaven, and resurrection means that the present world struggling under the oppression of sin will be redeemed. Resurrection is about turning the entire world upside down.[152]

The book of John is unique amongst the gospels because the author takes previously shared material in the previous gospels and reworks the information around several different themes.[153] One of those themes is immediately evident in the prologue of the gospel. John 1:1 echoes the wording of Genesis 1:1, as both books commence with "*In the beginning*". John continues to trace the theme of creation throughout his book. John declares that the Word is the source of all creation (1:3) that light pierces the darkness echoing the transition from darkness and void in Genesis to a world filled with light because of the spoken word from God. John 1 is written so that we may understand that Jesus is the source of all creation, but that source has come to dwell amongst us in human form (1:10, 14). The climax of Genesis 1 is the creation of man in God's image. The climax of John's prologue is the divine coming and dwelling amongst us in human form.[154]

The book of John contains seven miraculous events, the book of creation records seven day of creation (Genesis 1; John 2:1-11; 4:46-54; 5:2-9; 6:1-14, 16-21; 9:1-7; 11:1-44). When John begins to describe the resurrection of Jesus he begins in this way: "*Early on the first day of the week...*" (20:1). A seemingly innocuous statement, but John repeats himself a second time a few verses later: "*On the evening of the first day of the week...*" (20:19). Why would John twice in the same passage reiterate that it is the first day of the week? Because John is calling our attention once again to the Genesis story

[151] Wright, 2003. 32-84.

[152] Middleton, J. Richard. *A New Heaven and a New Earth: Reclaiming Biblical Eschatology*. Grand Rapids: Baker Academic, 2014. 154.

[153] Gundry, Robert. *A Survey of the New Testament*. Grand Rapids, Zondervan, 1994. 254.

[154] Wright, N.T. *The New Testament and the People of God*. Minneapolis: Fortress Press, 1992, 416.

of creation. In John 20:22 Jesus breathes on his disciples and tells them that they have received the Holy Spirit. In Genesis 1 the Spirit hovers over the formless earth. In Genesis 2 man is animated by the breath of God into his nostrils. John wants to tell us that the resurrection of Jesus is the first day of a newly created order. Much like the Genesis story attempts to explicate the meaning behind the created world, so too John wants his readers to know that new creation is happening amongst us. The resurrection means that the entire world is changing.

The resurrection of Jesus is the linchpin on which the entire course of history turns. For the apostle Paul if the resurrection is not a reality then we are better off simply enjoying the temporal pleasures of this earth because when we die there is no hope (1 Corinthians 15:32). Resurrection does not mean that our souls fly into heaven. This would mean that resurrection is no different than what is said to have happened to Caesar. Resurrection is the physical transformation of all things. Through the resurrection of Jesus our hope is tied not to angelic status floating away on the clouds. Rather our hope is that the creation that God called good in Genesis will one day be restored, redeemed, and rescued. The rocks, rivers, hills, mountains, trees, animals, and all the beautiful things God has created will be made whole once again. As theologian Jurgen Moltmann said:

> *"Men and women are not aspirants for angelic status, whose home is in heaven and who feels that on this earth they are in exile. They are creatures of flesh and blood. Their eschatological future is a human and earthly future—the resurrection of the dead and the life of the world to come. There are not two God's, a Creator God and a Redeemer God. There is one God. It is for his sake that the unity of redemption and creation has to be thought.*[155]

---

[155] Moltmann, Jurgen. *The Coming of God: Christian Eschatology*. Minneapolis: Fortress Press, 1996. 259. See also Moltmann, Jurgen. *Theology of Hope*. Minneapolis: Fortress Press, 1993. "*With the raising of Jesus all has not yet been done. The end of death's domination is still outstanding. The overcoming of all opposition to God is still outstanding in that future reality of which Paul says that 'God will be all in all'*". 163. Resurrection is not the end of history, rather it is a signpost for a future event in which all things will be subsumed in God and all things restored.

If the gospel accounts ended with the crucifixion of Jesus the story would end in despair. That is the situation at the end of the gospel of Luke where Jesus meets two companions on the road to Emmaus. As the two pilgrims make their way to Emmaus they meet Jesus on the road unaware of His true identity. They spend the seven mile journey together talking about the events of recent days, the ministry of Jesus, his crucifixion, and even of the rumors that the tomb where He was buried is now empty. They had such high hopes for the future, only to be let down in the end when the Romans executed Jesus. When they reach their destination they ask Jesus to eat dinner with them because the journey together was stimulating, and the teaching of their new friend has warmed their hearts. It is at this meal with the breaking of bread that Jesus true identity is revealed to them. Their eyes were opened and they recognize the risen Jesus, much like the eyes of Adam and Eve are opened when they ate of the forbidden tree in the Garden of Eden (Genesis 3:7; Luke 24:31). This meal happens to be the eighth meal scene in the gospel of Luke. The Last Supper is the seventh meal (Luke 22:7-23). The week of the first creation is over; with this meal the first day of new creation is inaugurated.[156]

For me, resurrection means all things will be made new.

There is no greater subject to me (Dino) than the resurrection. The heart of the Christian faith is the resurrection. Earlier in the book Jonathan spoke about his grandfather, my father, in the chapter entitled Legends. Jonathan never personally knew my father, but he has heard many stories about him because the family has retold many of their experiences of this man whom they dearly respected and loved. Resurrection means that there is coming a day when that legend will be together with my son and my other children. They will, in fact, see him.

With that in mind, I would like to address the resurrection in the following way. First, I would like to address the meaning of the event. Secondly, there will be a brief observation of the garments of Jesus, teaching amazing resurrection truth, and finally we will note briefly the recognition of the one true Lord based on this event.

Notice the meaning of the event. The resurrection of Jesus Christ teaches us that all who come by faith to Jesus Christ are justified

[156] Wright, N.T. *The Challenge of Jesus: Rediscovering Who Jesus Was and Is.* Downers Grove: InterVarsity Press, 1999. 146.

by Him. Sin has separated us from God and as desperately as we need to have a relationship with God there is recognition that we are incapable for such a desire to be fulfilled on our own. Without someone stepping into this situation and correcting it, we cannot have a relationship with God. The resurrection is the confirmation that the Father in heaven gives us access to a right relationship with Him. A part of this fact of justification is that death has been defeated. It is interesting that all people who have been on the earth will face death. Christ rose from the grave because death could not hold Him. Death is no longer an enemy. "*Where, O death is your victory? Where, O death is your sting?" The sting of death is sin, and the power of sin is the law. But thanks be to God! He gives us the victory through our Lord Jesus Christ*" (1 Corinthians 15: 55-57).

God the Father looks at believers as being a part of the union in Christ making us a family. This union is possible because of the resurrection of Jesus Christ. Believers in Christ may walk in newness of life. The outward demonstration of this walk is baptism. We go under the water briefly representing the death and burial of Jesus Christ, and then we are raised picturing the resurrection of our Lord.

The resurrection is the foundation of the truth of scripture. The fact that Jesus is alive today was Paul's argument throughout the book of Acts. In 1 Corinthians 15 the apostle Paul provides both a defense and a proclamation of the reality of the resurrection of Jesus Christ. The resurrection is the foundation of the message of Jesus.

"*...And who through the Spirit of holiness was appointed the Son of God in power by his resurrection from the dead: Jesus Christ our Lord*" (Romans 1:4). It is this resurrection that gives to believers around the world the hope of eternal life. The apostle Peter called it a '*living hope*' (1 Peter 1:3, 4).

Jesus rose. This truth is a precursor, prophesy, and prelude to all believers who one day will rise and be with the Lord. Christ will judge the world in righteousness. "*In the past God overlooked such ignorance, but now he commands all people everywhere to repent. For he has set a day when he will judge the world with justice by the man he has appointed. He has given proof of this to everyone by raising him from the dead*" (Acts 17:30-31). This miraculous event is the linchpin of Christianity and moves its message from law to grace, from works to deliverance, from hopelessness to eternal life.

The second item is the remarkable story of the resurrection itself. The story can be summarized and placed into any number of theories. One theory is that it really happened. Another theory is that the disciples were hallucinating. Another theory is that the resurrection is a myth. Perhaps Jesus did not really die but that he was swooned to sleep. None of these objections carry much evidence when compared to the reality. For example, if Jesus was swooned to sleep, why did the soldiers break the legs of the two thieves, yet they did not do the same with Jesus? They were convinced He was dead. That is the only reasonable explanation.

There are numerous such evidences. For now, let's consider the handkerchief that was around the head of Jesus. "... *As well as the cloth that had been wrapped around Jesus' head. The cloth was still lying in its place, separate from the linen*" (John 20:7).

> "*Theologically, the lying there of the linen wrappings and of the face-cloth shows that Jesus has taken up his life by his own initiative, under his divine power; nobody has had to unwrap him as Lazarus had to be unwrapped*" (11:44 compare 2:19; 10:18).[157]

I have led twenty trips to Israel. On the trips, there are many interesting lessons, and stories to pick up by the residents and community leaders. One such story is that when Peter and John came into the empty tomb, they saw the linen cloths lying there. The napkin that was neatly lying there reminded them of a custom. When a member of the royalty hosted a banquet, they would often lie on a couch. Occasionally, they would rise and go outside for some air. If they would not return, they would wipe their mouths and leave the napkin there, with no attention given to its appearance. If the master was to return, they would fold the napkin neatly and the servants would know to leave things as they are, for their leader was going to return. When Peter and John saw the napkin there folded neatly, they knew that Jesus would return. The custom and the placing of the napkin was most remarkable. He was, in fact, alive and somewhere near. Perhaps John was thrilled, and Peter felt

[157] Gundry, 1994, 288.

like he was such a failure that it did not matter. Little did Peter know of how God would use his life as the church age was about to begin.

My final thought is what does this miracle of the resurrection mean? C.S. Lewis wrote:

> *[Jesus] has forced open a door that has been locked since the death of the first man. He has met, fought, and beaten the King of Death. Everything is different because he has done so. This is the beginning of the new creation; a new chapter in cosmic history has opened.*[158]

We now need to think it through. How does that apply to me?

This is what it means to me. In a little memorial garden outside the town of Chambersburg, Pennsylvania are two memorial stones. One of the stones remembers Fred Pedrone, my father, Jonathan's grandfather. The other stone is in memory of Bertha Pedrone, my mother and Jonathan's grandmother. My parents are with Jesus. Paul the apostle spoke of those who have departed from this world and referred to this truth in Philippians 1:23, "*I am torn between the two: I desire to depart and be with Christ, which is better by far.*"

Paul's struggle was between staying here on the earth and going to be with Jesus. He wanted to be with Jesus. Where is Jesus? In Acts 1:11 we are told He went into heaven at the ascension. The Old Testament refers to heaven over 300 times and again over 250 times in the New Testament. The Greek word in the New Testament that is commonly used is *ouranos,* meaning God's dwelling place. My parents, because of their faith in Jesus Christ are now with Jesus. One day I will see them again. At the resurrection we have new bodies. The resurrection refers to a new world, new ruler, and new blessings.

The resurrection is the heart of the Christian faith. Jonathan said it so well. "The resurrection is the lynchpin on which the entire course of human history turns".

When that day of the resurrection occurs for all of us, I am looking forward too many things, including a nod to my son and saying "Hey Jonathan, over here! Meet your legendary grandfather."

---

[158] Lewis, C. S. *Miracles*. London: Collins, 2012. 247.

ACKNOWLEDGEMENTS

Every book is the result of the work of many different people. The authors would like to thank the following people specifically for their contributions to this work.

Cory J. Adams was a valuable help with technical issues surrounding this book.

Emerson and Rosina Brandon were our gifted editors and contributed numerous hours going over the text of the book. Because of their hard work the quality of this book was greatly improved upon.

Adam Pedrone created the cover for this book and all the art for this book. His ability to take our abstract ideas and convert them into a cover design is greatly appreciated. More of his exceptional work can be seen on his website: adampedrone-artdesign.com

Our families have supported each of us as we worked on this project. Their patience with us and willingness to provide us the space to study, research and write this book makes them unique contributors to this project.

Finally for all of our readers, we hope that we have opened up a conversation about the words of Jesus that will go beyond the text of this book.

Printed in the United States
By Bookmasters